EGYPTIAN ART

EGYPTIAN ART

BY WERNER AND BEDŘICH FORMAN • TEXT BY Dr MILADA VILÍMKOVÁ • TRANSLATED BY TILL GOTTHEINER • WITH A PREFACE BY MOHAMMED H. ABD-UR-RAHMAN, CURATOR OF THE EGYPTIAN MUSEUM IN CAIRO

PETER NEVILL • LONDON

PHOTOGRAPHS AND GRAPHIC DESIGN BY WERNER AND BEDŘICH FORMAN • DESIGNED AND PRODUCED BY ARTIA FOR PETER NEVILL • SPRING HOUSE · SPRING PLACE · LONDON NW5 • • PRINTED IN CZECHOSLOVAKIA

THE AUTHORS WISH TO THANK Mr MOHAMMED H. ABD-UR-RAHMAN, CURATOR OF THE CAIRO MUSEUM, WHOSE UNDERSTANDING AND SUPPORT MADE THIS BOOK POSSIBLE

W. and B. FORMAN

FOR A.S.H. CRAEYBECKX OF ANTWERP WHO DEDICATED HIS LIFE TO PHOTOGRAPHY

THE ROOTS OF OUR EUROPEAN CULTURE LIE DEEPLY EMBEDDED IN THE culture of Greece and Rome and without as much as realising it we still today enjoy the fruit whose sap rose long ago in antiquity. For us the form and content of Classical art are familiar and comprehensible. Many public buildings in our cities might serve as textbook examples of Greek or Roman architectural orders. Statues of Apollo and the Muses decorate our theatres, Roman trigae or quadrigae tower on triumphal arches, and light-footed Mercuries guard the entrances to stock exchanges and banks.

In everyday speech we use innumerable words of Greek or Latin origin without giving the matter a second thought. Antiquity has remained alive for us, even if at times only in our subconscious being. Europeans have consciously turned back to ancient philosophy and to the arts of antiquity at all great crossroads of history. Antiquity has influenced whole epochs of development: it provided European culture and art with new content and form at the time of the Renaissance; and as late as the end of the eighteenth century its influence was still strong enough to contain the exuberant Baroque within the quiet, if somewhat speculatively severe order of Classicism. In times of doubt nations and individuals have turned back to antiquity, and as a result our attitude to the art of Greece and Rome is today something natural and self-evident.

In sharp contrast to the living heritage of Greece and Rome, Egyptian culture suffered the strange fate of something gigantic but forgotten, hidden under the desert sands that piled up as the centuries passed, strange old tales born of ignorance, a mystery beyond comprehension. The traditions of antiquity may well be partly to blame for this attitude of Europeans to ancient Egypt—especially the literal imterpretation of accounts of ancient travellers who, in their descriptions of foreign countries, stressed what seemed to them strange and unaccustomed, and failed to take note where the foreign ways proved identical to their own. Furthermore, late antiquity took over from the spiritual heritage of Egypt the two mysterious cults of Isis and Osiris. The exotic character of their mysteries proved greatly attractive, and though in fact they had little in common with Egyptian religious cults they gave rise to the impression in European minds that anything even faintly connected with Egypt was mysterious and incomprehensible.

At the beginning of the last century educated Europeans still believed in the secrets of the Pyramids, in the profound and enigmatic symbolism of the hieroglyphic inscriptions, which at that time had still not been deciphered but were, notwithstanding, being feverishly interpreted. This mystery, on the one hand, provoked scepticism among those brought up in the classical tradition (Goethe, for instance, called Egyptian art 'the sacred twilight'); on the other hand, it attracted romantics. Beethoven had on his work-table one of the profound symbolic sayings: 'I am that which is here; I am all that has been and will be; no mortal has lifted my veil . . .' At that time the mysterious veil that had for so long hidden the face of ancient Egypt was gradually beginning to part, and after the long ages of semi-obscurity the culture of ancient Egypt suddenly became accessible. That long period is strangely linked with the campaigns of two great conquerors. Long ago, Alexander the Great sealed the fate of Egypt when he completed his conquest of the land of the Nile. Napoleon re-opened the gate to the knowledge of that gigantic art by his expedition to Egypt two thousand years later.

The deciphering of the hieroglyphic script provided the key. Here chance played its part. In 1799 French soldiers dug up in the neighbourhood of the village of Rosetta a stone slab with inscriptions engraved in hieroglyphics, demotic and Greek. After years of concentrated work the French scholar, Jean François Champollion, succeeded in deciphering the hieroglyphics recording the names of Greek rulers. In a letter to M. Dacier, in which he explained the basis of his discovery, Champollion laid the foundation of a new branch of learning, Egyptology. His pioneering work soon attracted followers, and today Egyptology can pride itself on many famous names—Lepsius, Mariete, Wilkinson, Flinders Petrie, Maspero, Erman, Turajev, Gardiner and many others, whose work enables us to read the hieroglyphic script instead of interpreting it symbolically. Today, almost every great museum in the world owns a collection that documents the whole development of Egyptian art.

One of the richest and most complete collections of Egyptian art is rightly that of the Cairo Museum. The selection in this book of reproduction of sculptures, reliefs and paintings from the Museum constitutes an outline of the development of that art (although by no means exhaustive) from the period of the IIIrd Dynasty, round about 2800 B. C. until the late period of the eighth and seventh centuries B. C.

Today, Egyptian art is not an entirely unexplored field for most educated people. But it can hardly be said that it has become as familiar as Greek or Roman art. It does not, and can not, penetrate so deeply into our lives—do we ever see Egyptian zoomorphological gods on our buildings? The one exception perhaps is the sphinx. Nor do we currently employ words taken over from ancient Egypt.

Egyptian art is, and undoubtedly will always remain, a matter for museums and books, or, at best, a subject of interest to a few private collectors. Though it has many patrons and admirers, it has remained an exclusive art, not as readily comprehensible as Greek and Roman art. This can be seen even in the views expressed by experts. To some it appears as the expression of a level of culture almost as advanced as that of Europe; others regard it as the expression of a certain primitivism. There are scholars who fully accept, for instance, the element of portraiture in Egyptian sculpture, while others deny this, claiming that Egyptian art did not achieve more in that sphere than the expression of certain racial features.

In view of all this I have felt that it would be useful to accompany this selection of examples from the Cairo Museum with brief notes, intended to facilitate an understanding of Egyptian art for those readers to whom at first sight some of these works may seem somewhat strange.

The period of three thousand years during which Egyptian art developed has often been compared to the mighty river Nile. There is something in this. Like the river, Egyptian art derived its inspiration from one source without coming under foreign influences. The creative strength of the one nation began and completed without foreign aid an enormous task, overcoming the difficulties of periods of unrest and renewing itself again and again from its own substance. The metaphor of the Nile is, in fact, more than a random choice. The river had a part in this remarkable achievement. The regular alternations of flood and drought gave the people who had come to settle in the Nile valley a regular rhythm of life right from the beginning. The mud brought down by the river guaranteed fertile land to all those who knew how to take advantage of the gift. The great river and the burning sun thus became the first organisers of human life and labour in the narrow valley enclosed on both sides by desert. And during periods of unrest it was again the river that annually reminded the disorganised land and its people that it was time to return to the affairs of daily life, since only careful attention to these would ensure the country's safety and well-being. The people of the Nile Valley very soon came to understand the discipline imposed by the river. As early as the third millennium B. C. they established an empire whose internal organisation facilitated the smooth and systematic execution of all work connected with the life-giving floods. The birth of the first, the Old Kingdom, marks the beginning of the historical era in Egyptian history. As we shall see, Egypt entered it with quite unusual determination and with an art already well developed.

Egypt, too, went through paleolithic, mezolithic and neolithic periods. The so-called pre-dynastic era already belonged to the fourth stage of development, the chalcolithic, when metal (bronze) tools made their appearance. There is very little among the somewhat monotonous collection of objects, mainly utensils, which were unearthed during the excavations of the older pre-dynastic settlements that points to future developments. From time to time pure, precisely shaped pots, spoons or small spades carved in ivory with a highly developed sense of form and decoration were found. The flint tools, worked with extraordinary care, or the basalt, alabaster and limestone vessels of noble shape are proof that even in times long past the people of Egypt had acquired the knack of handling materials that were difficult to fashion. Amongst all these objects the human figure played the rôle of Cinderella. Its shape, drawn or carved, was no further advanced than in other known prehistoric cultures, that is, the figures were basically no more than idols. Only on rare occasions were marks of sex given greater prominence.

Far surer in touch and closer to reality were some of the drawings and sculptures of animals, particularly statuettes of the hippopotamus.

Objects that were to become characteristic of the Ist Dynasty did not appear until the very last stage of prehistorical development. (These were found during excavations at El-Gerza.) They include palettes which served for grinding malachite, which was used as a make-up. Some of the palettes have the shape of birds or fish, others are heart-shaped or rectangular, curved at one end and covered with reliefs of tiny human figures or animals, at times chaotically scattered over the entire palette, at others arranged in rows one above the other. The production and use of these slate palettes continued into the proto-dynastic period, and it is certainly no accident that it was on one of them that the Egyptian artists managed finally to solve the problem of depicting human beings. This palette was Narmer's palette, which cannot have been an isolated work of its kind and was certainly not the first attempt at works of this type. An intermediary stage in the search for a solution can be seen on the fragment of a limestone capital of a cudgel of King Scorpion. The king is dressed in a kilt and wears a tall cap which in shape shows a development towards the White Crown of Upper Egypt. He holds an Egyptian hoe in one hand. Before him stands a scribe holding a scroll; behind him, servants with fans. The subject matter deals with the official beginning of the economic life after the Nile floods have receded, and the relief shows how closely, in its early stages, the kingship was linked with the administration of the region.

From a formal point of view there already existed in rough outline an indication of the pose which the maker of Narmer's palette borrowed. King Scorpion is depicted in profile but with his shoulders twisted *en face*. The artist who created Narmer's profile went, of course, much further. He subdivided the large area of the heart-shaped palette horizontally into self-contained registers of events which provided the basic scheme of composition. The human figure, too, had assumed the definite form that was to become characteristic of Egyptian art. The canon of proportions, it is true, was still somewhat uncertain—the body was too short in relation to the long, strong legs, the head on the short thick neck was thrust between the shoulders, the muscles of arms and legs were marked graphically, but already with clear differentiation as to anatomy (e. g. the left and right feet of the king and the servant carrying the sandals). But the palette was of significance for future development not only in its formal aspects. No less important were the events the artist depicted.

By a strange coincidence the artist preserved a piece of information of great historical interest. On the one side the king is depicted wearing the White Crown, his left hand grasping by the hair a kneeling, overpowered enemy. His right arm is held up high with a cudgel. The enemy, as we are told in the symbolic depiction in the top right-hand register of the palette, where the royal falcon is standing above a strange creature with a human head and body out of which papyrus reeds are growing, was the ruler of the northern territories of Egypt, the swampy region of the Nile delta.

On the other side of the palette, the artist continued his story: the king in the form of a strong bull destroys the enemy fortress and then, wearing the conquered Red Crown, triumphs over the defeated foe. In a brief, clear-cut manner these scenes relate a great historical event— the foundation of the Old Kingdom by the unification of Upper and Lower Egypt.

The union was effected by the King of Upper Egypt, Narmer, whose name is marked on the palette. This king was probably identical with the legendary founder of the Old Kingdom, Menes. We do not know whether this union was a permanent one from the very beginning. It is more likely that the struggle for control of the country went on throughout the first two dynasties, and that for a time the king of the North, Khasekhem, regained supremacy. Nevertheless, the course of development shows that by the IIIrd Dynasty a definite union had taken place, and that the internal administration of the country was well regulated. Otherwise it would hardly have been possible for the first sovereign of that Dynasty, Zoser, to have undertaken the gigantic building operations that link his name and the name of his leading architect, Imhotep, for ever with the fame of Egypt. The most famous period of the Old Kingdom was the time of the IVth Dynasty—the dynasty of the builders of the Pyramids, the kings Snefru, Khufu (Cheops), Khafre (Chefren), Menkawre (Mykerinos). The gigantic pyramids of these kings are living monuments to the absolute power these rulers must have exercised and to the advanced organisation of the country that with only primitive means and limited knowledge at its disposal managed, in the course of one generation—for each pharaoh had a pyramid built as his final resting place—to carry out a work that later came to be admired as one of the wonders of the world.

The rulers of the Vth Dynasty worshipped the sun god, Re, whose cult flourished in Lower Egyptian Heliopolis with its famous sun temple. The economic development of the country was under control, the kings undertook trade expeditions to the Land of Punt, whence they brought back myrtle and rare woods, and ventured as far as Syria, which yielded them timber for ship-building. The absolute power of the kings by degrees receded into the background and the caste of officials became more prominent. In the period of the VIth Dynasty these dignitaries became local rulers whose efforts to establish their sovereignty brought about a slow disintegration of the central system of government. The reign of the first king of the VIth Dynasty saw military successes against Nubia, but the power of the local rulers was growing and after the death of the last king of the Dynasty, Pepy II, who ruled for almost a century, the Egyptian lands were back where they had been at the beginning of the dynastic period—a conglomeration of independent but politically insignificant small states.

Egyptian art, perhaps more than the art of any other nation, faithfully reflects the economic and political conditions of the country. The flourishing development of Egypt in the period of the Old Kingdom greatly stimulated the arts. Already in the early period there were noticeable efforts towards precision and a definite stylisation of form. The Horus falcon, for example, which on Narmer's palette still had a small body with the big crop of a dove, changed into a magnificent bird on the stele of the King Serpent (Djet). Thenceforward, its silhouette remained unchanged for a millennium to come.

In the historical period this development was directly influenced by further factors that determined the content and form of Egyptian works of sculpture and painting. The first of these, one that principally affected the content of works of art, was the Egyptian belief in life after death—of course under conditions of proper burial. The form of their belief reflected the naive, literal manner of thinking of the old Egyptians, who imagined life after death as a replica of life on earth, with all its attendant pleasures, worries and needs. The body of the deceased had to be protected from decay, it had to be supplied with food, flowers, furniture and servants, in short, with everything to which the dead person had been accustomed in life. It was considered possible to provide everything in the form of pictures to which the validity of living persons or real objects was granted. The Egyptian sculptor was known by the fitting name of *sʿnch*, i. e. the one who infuses life. Pictures could be used as substitutes for the dead so that eternal life was ensured if a statue or picture in relief survived. As a result a great deal of what we know about Egyptian art today was made not for the rays of the burning sun but for the murky shade of the tombs. The second factor which greatly influenced the forms of art was the attempt to achieve absolutely clear and comprehensible depictions of visible reality. The feeling for the concrete, and the non-interchangeability of the picture, arose from the very basis of the hieroglyphic script, since in the initial stages of its development form and meaning were identical—the picture of the object meant the object itself. In the course of time the hieroglyphic script grew into a stylised shortland which, however, fully respected and preserved the clear observation of the characteristic form of the depicted person or object. From this point of view it is clear that Egyptian art rejected all that constituted an obstacle to the immediate and clear-cut identification of the picture, i.e. close similarity of form and perspective foreshortening.

For the depiction of most animals the artists selected the profile view, but in the case of sheep, goats and cattle the two horns were always shown *en face* (Plate 84), as it would not have been possible in profile to show their characteristic curves. In contrast, gazelles' horns were shown in profile, because only at that angle was their shape clearly visible. In the same manner the silhouettes of birds' bodies were more expressive in profile (Plate 8), only the head of the owl being given *en face* (cf. inscription to Plate 32), as in profile it would have lost its characteristic traits: the square shape of the head and the round eyes. Small animals that creep on the ground such as salamanders or insects, were depicted by the Egyptians from above, with the exception of snakes, whose most characteristic features were the curving of their bodies and the profile view of the head. This combination of typical angles of view was sometimes taken so far on reliefs and painting that we have difficulty in understanding the approach, so different from our modern conception. A detailed explanation of the Egyptian rules was attempted by the German Egyptologist, Heinrich Schäfer, in his work *Von ägyptischer Kunst*, in which, among other things, he turned to children's drawings for purposes of comparison. The conditions, he says, are approximately identical. The child, free from accepted ways of looking at things, is compared to the equally unprejudiced way of viewing objects of primitive man. This study reveals many interesting facts. Nevertheless, it has its shortcomings. The way a modern child looks at things and depicts them is not and cannot be absolutely immediate except in isolated instances. Here we are on uncertain ground as the approach of a child that is naturally gifted differs from that of a child who lacks a talent for art; nor can we ever know how much the young artist unconsciously derives from looking at picture-books. The results of experiments of this kind must take into account circumstances that cannot be objectively evaluated. On the other hand, the works of the Egyptian artists in the period of the first dynasties were no longer the expression of primitive man; on the contrary, they were already highly sophisticated works, in which the effects were fully calculated. It was not primitivism or a child-like vision that at times achieved such confused and topsyturvy effects, but concrete observation and the endeavour to achieve complete clarity. Most of us naturally appreciate the space around us as though looking at a ground plan and are capable of drawing a simple plan of this form—our own flat, for example. If into the plan we were to draw all vertical objects, i.e. doors, windows and furniture, all in their places, but at the same time seen in their characteristic appearance, i.e. no longer in plan but in normal outline, taking care, however, that they all fit into the plan, and if, finally, we were to add several figures of people drawn in profile, the result would be a largely chaotic picture. But it would be one that in manner of depiction would be very close to the Egyptian pictures in the royal palace at Tell-el-Amarna.

The search for complete clarity and lack of ambiguities in the depiction of objects influenced the Egyptian method of depicting the human figure in drawing and relief. Over a long period of development the human figure was shown from several characteristic angles. The head was traditionally drawn in profile, the eye from the front, the shoulders full-on in such a way that the body was given a twist so that the upper part was in profile with the right or left nipple shown (according to the twist) and the hips in three-quarter profile with (in the case of man) the navel clearly visible; the thighs were indicated only by curves and the legs given in full profile, frequently with inverse depiction of the feet, i.e. the big toes on the same side, usually the left ones, as the Egyptians preferred to depict the human figure from its right side with the left foot striding forward. The inclusion of other toes would have involved foreshortening and a consequent lack of clarity, which the Egyptians at all costs wished to avoid. This manner of depiction satisfied the demand for complete clarity and appealed to their aesthetic feeling. The human figure seen in profile has, from an artistic point of view, a somewhat indefinite shape around the shoulders and chest, faintly reminiscent of a full sack, which can only be given shape with difficulty. The effect of the broad shoulders in proportion to the narrow body gives a much nobler and more convincing picture of the body than would be the case in full profile.

This somewhat complicated and highly stylised posture, which has falsely been called impossible, crystallised into the archetype of the human figure in Old Egypt and was copied and re-copied in later dynasties. Masterpieces exemplifying this conception are the panels in Hesire's tomb (Plates 1—3, 6, 7). The very low relief shows the occupant of the tomb, the deceased official, Hesire, walking or sitting in front of a table with offerings, always in the same basic position, differentiated only by the movements of the hands. The eleven panels side by side suggest simple variations on a theme. The profile of Hesire's head is identical on all panels and undoubtedly incorporates elements of portraiture. The figure is idealised in its dry noble form with well-balanced proportions and delicate modelling of the surface. Very striking, even though stylised, is the anatomically correct indication of the bones and the modelling of the most important muscles to give an impression of exertion.

Hesire's panels are among the crowning works of the Egyptian creative spirit. In spite of the fact that, as we shall see, Hesire was copied innumerable times by later artists of the Old Kingdom, all replicas are but faint shadows of this work by an anonymous artist of the IIIrd Dynasty. On closer analysis Hesire's reliefs reveal quite considerable internal differences. It would appear that two artists shared in the work—master and disciple, perhaps. If we compare, for example, relief No. 1 with relief No. 6, we see that the latter has a much more general outline, is less expressive in its modelling of the body surface and is, as it were, simplified even in proportions, strikingly so in the excessively slim hips.

If we compare the reliefs of Hesire with the figures on the false door to the tomb of Eika (Plate 12), we can judge for ourselves how this generalisation of proportions progressed in the way indicated in relief No. 6. The proportion of the broad shoulders to the hips had changed. While, on the Hesire panel No. 1, the breadth of the shoulders corresponds roughly to twice that of the hips, on panel No. 6 the proportion is 1 : 2.2 and on the reliefs on the Eika door even 1:2.5—2.6. In relation to the thigh the navel is set much further down, and the outline is stressed by the use of intaglio relief. This is divided from the background only by an incision of the outline so that the crest of the curves on the relief remains on the same plane as the background. This technique seems to have involved less work, avoiding the difficulty of having to remove the layer of the background that corresponded to the height of the relief. It gained in terseness and expressiveness, the bones were no longer marked and the surface became more superficial, with the exception perhaps of the knees.

All these reliefs are official art, with a serious message, for they represent the deceased face to face with eternity. In such works the basic pattern and the canon of proportions were strictly adhered to.

What did the Egyptian artists do when they were not so completely bound by the sacred duties of their task? Clearly, the basic stylised picture of the human figure was used whenever the content demanded adherence to these conditions. The pattern could be used for a great number of variants, as shown by the scene of the fighting boatmen (Plate 32). Nevertheless, it often happened that the movement that was to have been shown went against the basic pattern. Hence, in scenes of daily life, with their endless diversity of movement, we find frequent deviations. The same applied to themes taken from work in the fields, hunting scenes, craftsmen in their workshops and events from public life. Notice, for example, the figures of the musicians (Plate 27). Here it will be found that the artist conformed to the classical pattern only in the drawing of the figure of the man playing the long pipe. Most of the other figures are depicted in full profile, as the movement involved in playing demanded.

On the other hand, the sculptor who carved the procession of men bearing offerings (Plate 18) had no reason to depart from the traditional manner. To depict the hand of a man carrying a vessel or basket so that it formed part of the figure involved no difficulties which might have meant sacrificing the convention. On the other hand, he did not hesitate to do so when the special character of the subject or reasons of composition demanded it. The figures of the gods on the reliefs of the funerary temple of King Sahure (Plates 15—17, 28) have only one arm, and it would appear that the second arm was left out purely for compositional reasons. The artist, not wishing to give the second hand a function, simply omitted it. In comparing all these reliefs it becomes clear that there were two lines of approach: the strict application of traditional patterns for official works and the ability to digress from that convention in scenes showing real life.

Bas-relief and painting were not the only media used by Egyptian artists, although it might be said that under certain circumstances they were their most spontaneous form of expression. By the side of flat depiction free-standing sculpture and architecture developed. Like relief, both were aimed at the basic types or patterns. In architecture there was a striving for pure geometrical form that crystallised in the pyramid, the search for clear-cut expression of mutual relations of support, and cross-beams with stress on the supports, and finally the attempt to achieve clear and organic spatial arrangement.

In sculpture, where the main emphasis was again on the human figure, two types were already formed in the early period: these were basically in harmony with the single-plane depiction. The official sculptures of the human figure to begin with had only two variations: the Egyptian sculpture hewed out of stone or carved in wood either seated figures—usually on a throne or some other seat with a tall back-rest—or a standing figure, also with a tall stone slab reaching to the shoulders at the back. This was not just an element of composition but mainly a structural support for the standing figure. The posture corresponded to the official pose of the reliefs —usually with the left leg striding forward, and differing only in the position of the arms. The body of the sitting figure usually followed the angles of the seat, the legs were placed side by side on the pedestal, and again the only variant possible was the position of the arms.

The third variation typical of Egypt and somewhat closer to the genre is the depiction of the scribe sitting cross-legged with a scroll of papyrus unrolled on his lap (Plates 21, 22). Finally, there is the heroic depiction, the sphinx, the recumbent body of a lion with a human head. This last type of sculpture could be used only for a ruling pharaoh.

This classification applied to official portraiture. If the scale seems somewhat limited, one has only to look at some of the official monuments of today to discover that the basic conception of representational sculpture has not changed greatly since the days of Old Egypt. Since such sculptures usually portray their subjects in postures of alert repose, the modern era knows only two alternatives: the sculptor can design a monument of a seated or a standing person; and, as the equestrian statue is no longer encouraged, *tertium non datur*. The choice open to Egyptian sculptors was in a way wider than to their modern counterparts.

The tradition of statues of seated sovereigns goes back to the period of the Ist Dynasty. The statues of King Khasekhem, a ruler of the IInd Dynasty, represent a man wrapped in a tight-fitting cloak, sitting on a low-backed throne. The White Crown on his head already has its typical conical shape that remained unchanged in later periods. The figure of the king follows the angles of the throne precisely, only his back is bent slightly forward. The clenched fist of the right hand rests on the right knee, the left lies across the lap with the palm lying flat on the right forearm.

Another link in the tradition is the statue of King Zoser (IIIrd Dynasty) which, in contrast to that of Khasekhem, is deeply merged into the block, the lower part of the king's body being enclosed by the side-rests of the throne. The ruler wears a royal wig-cover (*nemes*) over his heavy wig, which had not yet achieved full classical form. A ceremonial beard adorns his chin.
The flat palm of the left hand is resting on his knee, the right, with clenched fist, is held against the breast.

A perfect example of a composition on this theme is the diorite statue of one of the famous pharaohs of the IVth Dynasty, King Chefren (Plate 11). In contrast to his predecessors, Chefren is dressed only in a short pleated kilt, while the upper part of his body is naked. The head is covered in a royal wig-cover in its fully developed form with striped ends hanging down to below the shoulders in front. He sits in a majestic, stiff pose on a throne with a back-rest reaching to his shoulders. The axial symmetry of the frontal view is stressed by the identical position of the hands, the right one resting on the right knee, the clenched fist holding a folded kerchief, the left hand flat on the left knee. The profile view is dominated by the Horus falcon standing on the back of the throne and enfolding the king's head from behind with its open wings. The flat sides of the throne, against which the legs stand out in relief, show ornamental plant reliefs symbolising the union of Upper and Lower Egypt. Chefren's figure is an embodiment of the idealised form mentioned earlier in connection with bas-relief: broad muscular shoulders, arched chest, flat abdomen and slim hips.

So far we have only dealt in general terms with the Egyptian manner of depicting the human figure, without mentioning one of the most important aspects, the face. It has already been noted that opinions as to portraiture in Egyptian sculpture differ. In some cases the portrait seems an indisputable fact; the question, however, remains whether those are not exceptional works having little in common with the average run of works of their period. This would lead one to the conclusion that the portrait was a more or less accidental achievement of a particular artist who had surpassed his environment, i.e. that it was the product of his individual skill and not a sign of a general attempt to depict the human face faithfully. The question of portraiture, or rather the degree of portraiture, in Egyptian sculpture is, in the writer's opinion, an important one which deserves consideration in greater detail.

To begin with, what do we actually understand by the term 'portrait'? A fitting and simple, if somewhat general, definition was given by Schäfer: 'A portrait is a depiction that gives us the convincing impression that the maker wished to catch the features of a living person for their own sake.' Part of the definition is actually a pre-condition and we might therefore pose the question: did the conditions exist in Old Egypt that would enable the artist—usually the sculptor—to express a desire 'to catch the features of a living person for their own sake'? That brings us back to the basic impetus, the origin and development of Egyptian art. If we understand the reason why the Egyptian sculptors fashioned the human figure out of a block of stone or a tree trunk, we shall come to the conclusion that in theory those conditions did exist in Egyptian art, more so than in the art of any other country. The Egyptian had his portrait made, and the sculptor made it, at the express wish of the customer, since his likeness, carved in stone or wood, was the bearer of eternal life and the guarantee of continued existence. So that no mistake might creep in, the sculptures were marked with the name of the person they depicted. One might say, and it is often said in connection with Egyptian art, that the primitive attitude was satisfied when *any* form was identified with a name. Certainly, during the primitive stage of development it would have been sufficient to attach a name to an idol of the simplest form. On the other hand such a primitive stage would have had to be sufficiently advanced to be proficient in expressing thoughts in writing. At the period of the IIIrd Dynasty, as the Hesire panels show, Egyptian artists were able to create works of a high standard of sensibility with a firm structure of stylised and aesthetic principles. Admittedly, like the human figure, the face, too, might have been idealised to comply with aesthetic principles and rules of stylisation, but one can hardly accept the idea that the face might have been a random one. The basis of portraiture deserves more profound thought. What constitutes a portrait? What is it that convinces us that the artist wished to depict the face of a certain person and did so at his express wish? The answer is that the secret of portraiture lies in the faithful depiction of those features that are most characteristic of a face and are sometimes stressed and made more explicit. In a frontal view this has mainly to do with the shape of the face—a sensitive expression of the parts around the mouth, chin and eyes; and the characteristic line of the profile is determined mainly by the shape of the nose. The secret of portraiture lies in the correct depiction of these features, while a humorous exaggeration leads to caricature. Everything else more or less complements the picture of a human face and can be stressed or suppressed according to need. In the parts around the mouth the most important features are the mouth itself—the shape of the lips, their outline, and above all the line of the closed lips, dividing the upper from the lower lip—and the plasticity of the muscles of the cheeks around the mouth.

In the case of the eyes, their shape is given *a priori*, but in each individual the nuances provide an opportunity for a highly sensitive appreciation of shape. Other points to be taken into consideration are the inner and outer corners that determine the position of the eye, the width of the upper lid, the line of the brows, and, in plastic depiction, the modelling of the lower lid. Among these general features some details are more important than others, varying from case to case. Their portrayal depends, among other things, on the artist's skill and the material he uses. Clay requires different treatment from marble or limestone or other hard materials, such as granite, that are difficult to fashion. A completely different approach is needed for wood, for example. All these facts have to be taken into account before a final conclusion can be reached. Only a detailed analysis of a given work from all points of view can at least approximately determine the true degree of portraiture that has been achieved.

The task becomes less difficult when we have the chance of comparing a number of different portraits of one person. All portraits of Beethoven, for instance, though differing from one another, have certain traits in common which are the most characteristic of Beethoven's face. The problem becomes more difficult where there are few such opportunities for comparison, and highly complicated where none exist. This complete lack of material applies to the sculptures of the Old Kingdom. With the exception of a few rare cases, each portrait is a unique work, having no duplicate. Leaving aside for a moment royal portraits, the most important of which are several statues of Chefren, let us turn to less official sculpture.

Among the outstanding examples of sculpture of the early IVth Dynasty are the well-known statues of Prince Rahotep and his wife, Princess Nefert (Plates 4 and 5). The faces of these two statues, at first glance, make an uncommonly lively, or rather lifelike impression, but nonetheless one is inclined to ask what their value is as portraits; to what extent did the artist wish to show the real appearance of husband and wife? To what degree was he able to do so? How far did he succeed?

Let us first examine the mouths. Both have mouths with broad full lips ending in blunt rounded corners. The line of the closed lips is hardly differentiated at all, falling slightly from the centre and levelling out at the corners in short horizontal lines. The furrows along the nose are given in an overall manner; under the corners are the slightly bulging muscles of the mouth. A mouth of this shape has few individual features—it can be found in almost every contemporary sculpture. It differs little from the mouth of Chefren or of some of the 'reserve heads'.

Now turn to the eyes. They are almost identical on both statues, indicated by the high curved line of the upper lids and the barely noticeable bent line of the lower lids, fusing again in the lightly elongated outer corners. The fold of the upper lid is a mere touch; the brows are placed high above the root of the nose, dropping gradually towards the temples; in the case of Nefert they end in a faint curve. We have seen such eyes already on the Hesire reliefs. They are repeated on the face of Chefren, and if we were to seek further comparison we should find eyes of this shape on most of the statues of the Old Kingdom. It might be said that the shape of the eyes is so general and undifferentiated that they can be likened to the hieroglyphic symbol *ir*—eye set in a human face. In other words, the most characteristic parts of the face are presented in both statues in a superficial manner. The eyes are stylised, the mouth betrays racial features rather than individual ones. The bearers of offerings on the reliefs (Plate 18) represent the same racial type as Prince Rahotep. And yet it must be admitted that the sculptor tried hard to create individual differences. Prince Rahotep is characterised not only by the small moustache on the upper lip but also by the marked furrow, or rather protuberance of wrinkled skin above the nose, which the sculptor modelled on the forehead, and by the broad chin and high cheek-bones.

In the case of Nefert the modelling stresses the soft, almost spongy roundness of the face while the marking of the furrow along the nose adds a slightly embittered expression. By mingling in this interesting manner individual, racial and stylised features, the maker of the two statues went half way towards depicting a real likeness. His aim was to achieve the most lifelike effect possible, and in this he was fully successful. The eyes, made up of transparent and semi-transparent stones to resemble the white, iris, pupil and cornea, give a convincing impression of life in spite of the stylised shape. Polychromy hid the lack of individuality by a pretence of real life.

In conclusion, we might sum up as follows: the artist who made the statues of Rahotep and

Nefert succeeded eminently in expressing racial type and achieved a convincing picture that appears true to life. He did not succeed in catching the real appearance fully though there are certain indications that he set out to do so. Both faces reveal a combination of racial features, individual traits and stylised elements.

The question remains whether this conclusion is generally valid for Egyptian sculpture of the Old Kingdom. The answer might be that it is indeed valid for most works of average or above-average accomplishment. From that period, however, some exceptional portraits in sculpture have also survived which truly deserve to be labelled portraits in the fullest sense of the word. One of these is the statue of Prince Hem-On in the Pelizäusmuseum at Hildesheim. The portrait shows the prince with a strikingly thin, bent nose, not unlike a bird's beak, and narrow lips in a full face which, unfortunately, is restored around the eyes. The prince's face differs completely from what might be called the Egyptian racial type and the sculptor undoubtedly managed to impart to the stone the real features of the deceased.

Another example of Old Kingdom portraiture is the masterly bust of Prince Ankh-haf, now in Boston. It is all the more interesting as it does not go beyond the racial type. It is exceptional for the expressive and anatomically correct modelling of the bones of the face and the skull. The arch above the eyes, the break in the line of the temples, the protruding cheek-bones and the shape of the skull can only have been observed from a living model. Similarly skilful is the modelling of the musculature of the face. The sculptor went even so far as to depart from the traditional stylisation of the eyes. The bust of Prince Ankh-haf is perhaps the only statue from the Old Kingdom where the eyes are not in the usual beautiful 'hieroglyphic' form but those of a real person, with clearly modelled upper and lower lids and sensitively modelled adjacent parts.

Among a number of other statues, none of which achieved the same degree of realism as the bust of Ankh-haf, there should also be mentioned the famous statue of the Scribe in the Louvre, the two statues of Ranofer in the Cairo Museum and the no-less well-known statue of the Sheik el-Beled, Ka-aper (known usually as the Village Sheik), also in the Cairo Museum (Plates 19 and 20).

Ka-aper is a plump, prosperous looking man, a type that seems to have been less common in the Old Kingdom than it is today. The stout figure with the paunch and strong legs is modelled to perfection, in spite of a certain terseness in the handling of detail. The fat man's face is true to racial type and yet shows a multitude of individual traits. The mouth is finely modelled, with striking curves of the closed lips, a natural line of the upper lip and a soft transition from the lower one to the adjacent parts. The fine dents at the corners of the mouth no longer follow the schematic curved outline. Equally characteristic is the aquiline nose with the broad nostrils. The sculptor followed the traditional manner only in the fashioning of the eyes. The latter, formed in a similar manner to those of Rahotep and Nefert of a combination of transparent and semi-transparent stones, kept the current 'hieroglyphic' shape with the formal indication of the folds of the upper lids. The statue of the Sheik-el-Beled shows that the ideal pattern of a slim, broad-shouldered man's figure did not bind the artist and that he could depict reality as he saw it. The extent to which the artists of the Old Kingdom were allowed and knew how to depart from the tradition of idealisation can be seen in a little group representing the dwarf Seneb and his family (Plate 35). Such family groups were a very popular genre in Egyptian art and can be traced throughout Egyptian history from the period of the Old Kingdom until a very late date.

The family group of the dwarf Seneb is a small sculpture, a circumstance that in itself might have led to the adoption of a well-tried scheme. The Egyptian sculptor, however, managed to depict the likeness and figure of the dwarf with admirable, almost naturalistic interest in the bizarre distorted proportions of the head to the trunk and limbs of the deformed body. Seneb sits beside his wife in a simple block seat, the little legs, like those of a child, are crossed below the powerful body, the short weak arms folded across the chest. The strong body supports an even more powerful, shapeless head. Portraiture must be sought in the shape and proportions of the body rather than in individual features. The eyes, for example, both of the dwarf and of his wife, are absolutely identical, as is the faint smile on both faces. The face of Seneb's wife is modelled in a much more superficial manner with less attention to real form. The relationship of husband and wife is suggested in a customary gesture of Egyptian art: the wife embracing her husband with her right arm around his shoulders and her left grasping his arm. The space in front of the seat is filled with the figures of Seneb's children.

The two little figures are conceived as compositional elements. But on closer examination it becomes clear that the Old Kingdom sculptor achieved something that was extremely rare in that early stage of development, namely the modelling of the figures of children in correct proportion, not merely as minute figures of adults, as had been customary in ancient times and in periods following. The little boy with the child's lock and the little girl with the short hair have plump bodies and their fingers pressed to their lips are real plump little children's fingers. The modelling of their hands is somewhat stiff, not like that of their mother's hands. It would appear, then, that the two children were intended to be much more than mere compositional elements and that the sculptor clearly enjoyed modelling them. This smiling family group in a curious way recalls our own old family photographs. The two children seem to say: 'Look what beautiful, charming and well-grown children the deformed dwarf Seneb has brought into the world.'

Let us return to the statues of the pharaohs of the Old Kingdom. None of the faces of the kings is depicted in stone with such lifelikeness and such evident signs of portraiture as the faces of their subjects carved in wood or stone. There is a striking difference between the art of the court and what we might call secular art, even though the destination of both was identical. The face of Chefren or Mykerinos, just like the faces of the well-known statues of the kings of the Vth and VIth Dynasties, show a far greater degree of stylisation and fever individual traits. This might be because, in the first place, the sculptors had only limited opportunities of getting close to their models and, secondly, because the kings of the Old Kingdom mostly had their statues carved out of the 'eternal' stones—hard granite and diorite. The material itself demanded smooth large areas, fewer nuances in transition and more definite outlines. Mottled granite almost excluded any fine gradation of the surface; the artist had to take into account the mottled colours that appear to break up any unified form. An example is the colossal statue of King Veserkaf (Plate 24), modelled in large surfaces and with clearly defined details. The mouth and the comparatively weak chin were perhaps the only real traits of the king.

The period of the VIth Dynasty saw a gradual decline in the powerful position of the Old Kingdom, a weakening of its internal organisation and a falling off in its art, which had risen to such heights in the IIIrd, IVth and Vth Dynasties. In sculpture traditional schemes were endlessly repeated (cf. Plates 30, 31, 33); it lost its monumentality and became genre in character, even in the statues of the pharaohs. These were signs of a worsening of political and social conditions in the Egyptian state. The VIth Dynasty was the last of the Old Kingdom and it was followed by a period of confusion, when power passed into the hands of local rulers. The disorganised state of the country tempted Asiatic tribes to invade the Nile delta, and the internal uncertainty and dissatisfaction finally burst out into social revolution.

The proverb '*Inter arma silent musae*' is more appropriate, perhaps, to Egyptian art than to the art of any other nation. The only possible exception is literature, since elegiac complaints about the fate of the country lying in confusion as the result of internal unrest and foreign invasions first appear during this period. While it may be easy to imagine a prophet lamenting over the ruins of a town, it is less easy to visualise a sculptor sitting amid those same ruins and carving a statue of his king out of granite or some other 'eternal' stone. In order to develop, Egyptian art needed a background of settled conditions, a wealthy class of officials, priests and other dignitaries whose assured position and economic prosperity were a guarantee for the peaceful work of the labourers building the tombs and the artists decorating the walls, and which gave the sculptors time to curb their unyielding material and the jewellers sufficient peace for their patient and precise work with gold and semi-precious stones. At times, however, when the Nile flooded its banks and the people could not plough, when they went to plough under the protection of a shield, or when pestilence raged in the country and the man who before had not even made sandals now became a wealthy master, there were not and could not be flourishing arts. This confused state of affairs, which lasted for more than a century and a half, culminated in a struggle between the local rulers of Herakleopolis and those of Thebes. In this fight for supremacy in Egypt, the rulers of Thebes emerged victorious, and after the middle of the twenty-second century B. C. they founded the XIth Dynasty with its seat at Thebes. This dynasty was the first of the Middle Kingdom, when power in Egypt was once again concentrated in the hands of sovereign kings. The country achieved its greatest prosperity under the pharaohs of the XIIth Dynasty. Those energetic rulers improved the economic conditions of the country by expanding the irrigation system, as a result of which large areas of arable land were reclaimed in the Faiyum oasis. The southern frontiers of Egypt were protected by several expeditions to Nubia; trade contacts with the south were made easier by the digging of a canal through the granite cliffs of the First Cataract of the Nile. The country, ruled over by a firm hand, once again enjoyed wealth and prosperity and could provide the required leisure for the exacting undertakings of its art-loving and gifted children.

To begin with it appeared that the Egyptian artists went a long way back in search of the road that had been buried and interrupted during the time of troubles. The statue of King Mentuhotep II, for example, with its enormous heavy legs gives an impression, in comparison with the slim elegant figures of the rulers of the Old Kingdom, of a clumsy primitive experiment. Another group of artists followed up the genre types of the VIth Dynasty. The statuette of Queen Ashayet, for example, hardly differed at all from the small statues of women bearing offerings. The faces of the kings of the XIth and early XIIth Dynasties were mainly stylised and individual traits largely suppressed.

The surviving monuments show that the main emphasis in art had changed. While the artists of the Old Kingdom had managed to get very close to men in what we may call private portraits, all their attention in the Middle Kingdom was centred on the personality of the ruler. In number and artistic form the statues of the kings far exceeded those of private persons. Similarly, in relief, increasing importance was attached to the king and his deeds, and to his court.

Relief decoration and drawings followed the traditions of the Old Kingdom by taking over without change the classical scheme of depicting the human figure. The reliefs on the sarcophagi of Queen Kawit and Queen Ashayet show, however, that the artists chose a new canon of proportions, not very different from that of the earliest period, as shown on the Narmer palette. The figures on the reliefs are tall and slim, with small heads and long legs quite out of proportion to the short trunk. Typical is the dry restrained modelling of the surface with precise, almost scrupulous elaboration of the silhouette. In spite of the interesting and truthful observation of detail, as, for instance, the hands of the servant fixing the loose curl on the queen's wig (Plate 27), the reliefs leave rather a cold impression and lack vitality.

There was little in the art of the early Middle Kingdom to foreshadow in any way the fact that the end of that epoch would constitute one of the crowning periods in Egyptian sculpture. The faces on the statues of the kings of the XIth and the early XIIth Dynasties, compared to those of the Old Kingdom, seem a hopeless step backward. Their modelling is on the whole indifferently carved, the eyes have the current 'beautiful' shape, sometimes stressed by emphasis on the line of make-up used to extend the outer corners and the brows towards the temples. The mouth has the traditional form with rounded corners. The straight line of the closed lips is slightly raised at the corners and gives the face just the hint of a relaxed smile. This is mainly true of the statues of Amenemhet I and some of those of his son and successor, Sesostris I. Among several surviving statues of the latter we find some where certain individual traits stand out. The eyes, though conceived in the 'beautiful' shape, are set rather strikingly on the slant and contrast with the brows, which are placed high above the nose and drop noticeably towards the temples. Another individual feature of the face is the strong broad double-chin. We possess too little material for a comparison of the quality of the portraiture in Amenemhet II's statues. The two colossal sphinxes of that ruler—one in the Louvre, the other in Cairo—are monumental masterpieces, but do not deviate from the established tradition. The face is smoothly modelled in large patches, the eyes keep to the traditional 'beautiful' form, the mouth with its full lips, rounded corners and sharply defined edge is finely modelled but lacks any clearly individual character. The artist who carved this sphinx aimed at a balanced composition and an expression of dignified tranquillity in the face, while portraiture receded into the background.

We possess hardly any more information about the appearance of Sesostris II. The three over life-size statues show a common trait in the strikingly small, slightly pouting mouth set in a broad, short face.

After this uncertain prelude some of the portraits of Sesostris III and his son, Amenemhet III, appear as a most striking advance. Both father and son were strong rulers; both were exceptionally interesting as people. The father, a warrior and conqueror, the model of the legendary ancient hero, of whom stories were told for generations to come; the son an administrator, who initiated great irrigation projects and monumental architecture, whose name is associated with the legendary labyrinth in the Faiyum oasis, once counted among the wonders of the world. Both were energetic, though strikingly different in temperament. These traits can, in the author's opinion, be detected in the portraits of the two kings as they were preserved so many times for eternity by the Egyptian sculptors.

Not all statues of the two kings are of equal artistic merit. Among the portraits of Sesostris and of his son there are a few masterpieces which were a thousand years ahead of the sculptured portraits of their time, and in which all that remains of the old tradition is the use of wig-covers. One of the most beautiful portraits of Sesostris is the granite head of the statue in the British Museum. The king's face in no way resembles the smooth, uncertain faces of his predecessors. It is expressively modelled, with clear distinction between the bone and muscular structure of the face. The mighty forehead with the sharply defined edge passes into the depression of the temples, the expressive arches above the eyes have an almost vertical curve at the temples. The eyes with the heavy, broad, seemingly fatigued eyelids have nothing in common with the tradition of the 'beautiful' eye. The face with its broad cheek-bones is furrowed by deep lines down the nose, and the facial muscles around the mouth and the 'muscle of pride' on the energetic chin are clearly indicated. The drooping corners of the mouth give a slightly embittered expression. The sculptor, who undoubtedly faithfully reproduced the real appearance of the king's face, threw aside all the fetters of tradition. And as a great artist he went even further. He managed to imprint upon that face of dark granite something unfathomably spiritual that fills us with deep admiration. Even after several millennia the features of the king radiate unbroken will-power, pride, bitterness and the weary disdain typical of the mighty of this earth.

If we knew nothing about Sesostris III, one look at that face would suffice to indicate that he must have been an exceptional personality, and that the sculptor was one of the few who were worthy to be called upon to preserve for all times the face of such a king.

Almost as striking as the British Museum head is the grey granite head from Medamud in the Cairo Museum. It is not quite so strong in expression, but it has the same remarkable modelling of the sensitive, melancholic mouth. The maker of the statue, once part of the Carnarvon Collection, imprinted on Sesostris' face a strange expression of alleviated sorrow. The fragment contains something mysterious, difficult to express, which perhaps can only be found in one other model in the world—the death mask of Beethoven.

On the small fragment at Hildesheim the king's eyes are modelled so expressively that the fragment was positively identified merely from the upper part of the face. We have spoken of the works of great masters. The characteristic features of Sesostris' face—the eyes with the broad lids and the mouth with the down-drawn corners—are found in all his portraits, even in the least successful. Comparison and analysis of all the portraits definitely attributed and those not yet identified leads one, usually, to definite conclusions. Thus, for example, the problematic obsidian head in the MacGregor Collection, long considered a work of the later period, cannot be anything but a portrait of Sesostris III. A comparison with the London head and the grey granite head in Cairo offers convincing proof.

A number of portraits of Amenemhet III resemble those of his father. At first sight it seems that they lack that surprising identity of characteristic features so typical of the statues of Sesostris III. A far greater variety exists. While Sesostris III survived only in traditional portrayal with royal wig or crown, his son appears in novel iconographic forms. In the first place, the face of the royal sphinx is framed by a lion's mane instead of a wig-cover, and there exists a statue of the king in the guise of a priest wearing a rich wig. Let us first examine those portraits which, from an iconographic point of view, are in the old accepted tradition. There are two heads, both larger than life-size, the first in the British Museum, the second in Cairo. At first sight it seems that the Egyptian artists, after a short interval of realism, had returned to the 'beautiful' form, the smooth surfaces and imperceptible transitions. It is an undeniable fact that the sculptor idealised the king's face to a certain extent. But he idealised a real face with all its characteristic traits. Its individuality is not spoilt by stylisation in the overall 'beautiful' fashion. The London portrait, in particular, is a fine example of classical virtuosity by virtue of its fine smooth form and composition, while at the same time maintaining and differentiating the bone structure and muscles of the face.

Apart from those two heads we possess several others of the pharaoh with the royal wig-cover: the limestone statue from Hawara, now in the Cairo Museum, with its rather superficial carving of the eyes, and the small serpentine head at Cambridge, depicting the young king in a manner reminiscent of the Greek athletes of the VIth century B. C. Close to these in their idealised classical conception are the two well-known portraits with the White Crown, one in granite in the Cairo Museum (Plate 38) and one in basalt at Copenhagen. In the execution of the lower sections of the face both heads are related to the London head. The almond-shaped eyes with the broad lids and the slight elongation of the outer corners reveal a new concept of the stylised 'beautiful' form. These heads are undoubtedly portraits of the pharaoh in his youth; the granite head in Cairo, especially, gives the impression of a very young face.

Amenemhet's sphinxes form a special group. Unfortunately, only in some of them is the face well preserved. The sphinx in Plate 39 is very close in conception to the basalt head in Copenhagen, but shows less detail and has a more powerful expression. The same is true of the head of the statue of the king as a priest, found at Tanis (Plates 43 and 44).

During the period of the Middle Kingdom both progress and all that was finest in the old tradition can be seen in monumental sculpture, which was exclusively concerned with statues of the rulers of the land. Secular sculpture, in contrast with that of the Old Kingdom, only rarely reached the level of official art. The patterns of the Old Kingdom remained in everyday use. Preference was given to the 'eternal' stones, but colour, which had given to the statues of the Old Kingdom their appearance of lifelikeness, seems to have lost its significance. A new variation of the old type was the statue of a seated man wrapped in a long tight cloak which he clutched to his chest with both hands. In addition, the Middle Kingdom saw the creation of a new iconographic form, the 'block statue'. This was a statue of a man sitting on the ground with raised knees, with his arms crossed over them and the whole body wrapped tightly in a cloak. This block form enclosing the human body in a cube, on which the smooth surface, broken only by undulating lines indicating the limbs, could be used for long engraved inscriptions, remained popular until a very late date. Portraiture does not seem to have assumed any great importance in the secular art of the Middle Kingdom.

Nevertheless, even here, exceptions can be found: for example, the woman's head carved in wood (Plate 29—enlarged about three times). This is dated, according to the place of excavation near the pyramid of Sesostris I, from the early part of the XIIth Dynasty. It is such an exceptional work, however, that it is difficult to judge whether the dating is correct. The special treatment of the wig with the inlaid gold squares might even point to a slightly earlier period; the slanting almond-shaped eyes with the artificially prolonged outer corners were current during the middle part of the XIIth Dynasty. In any case, exact dating is not essential. This little head is a timeless work of art. The woman the Egyptian artist has portrayed is not beautiful; she has broad cheek-bones, a rather large, somewhat crudely shaped nose and the modelling of the excessively large eyes is superficial. The secret of the face lies in the mouth. The

Egyptian sculptor of the XIIth Dynasty had managed to catch that strange, almost hidden half-smile, the smile that is found on the faces of some of Leonardo da Vinci's women. And I suggest in all seriousness that what the Egyptian artist caught in wood, some time at the beginning of the second millennium B. C., found no parallel until the Mona Lisa. For it is the same mouth, the same smile.

A brief survey of the art of portraiture in Egyptian sculpture from the beginning of the Old Kingdom until the end of the Middle Kingdom might lead us to these conclusions:

From the schematic handling of the human face, which the artist of the early period of the Old Kingdom depicted mainly according to what he knew rather than what he saw, Egyptian art gradually developed toward the delineation of individual features. This applied primarily to the silhouette of the profile in relief, and the modelling of the mouth and the adjacent parts in free-standing sculpture, where the artists tried to differentiate the individual from uniform generalities. Individual features gradually became more prominent; on some of the best heads from the Vth Dynasty we see characteristic lines even in the modelling of the face. Only in the eyes was the traditional formula retained.

Progress was suddenly interrupted and, for a time in the confusion of the transitional period, development came to a complete standstill. During the XIth and the early XIIth Dynasties Egyptian art seemingly returned to its starting-point. Though the artists must have been completely fettered by tradition, lacking any freedom of expression, they made great efforts once again to free the human personality expressed in their statues from the monotony of identical shapes. We can follow this interesting process step by step in the portraits of the kings of the XIIth Dynasty. The character of the face changed with the adoption of a new position for the eyes; gradually the traditional scheme for the mouth was abandoned. Emphasis was placed on the bone structure of the face, which was differentiated from the soft muscular parts. And then, as if by a miracle, these achievements suddenly came to a climax in the sculptured portraits of the last kings of the XIIth Dynasty, Sesostris III and Amenemhet III. All that remained from the past was the royal wig-cover framing the face, and formulae that had been repeated century after century were thrown overboard.

If some of the portraits of Sesostris were works of almost crude realism, which were not so much attempts to reproduce the physical appearance of the king but to express his inner being, then the portraits of Amenemhet III were an attempt to re-create the 'beautiful' form, not, however, in the tradition of the preceding millennium but in the idealisation of observed reality. The Middle Kingdom was the end of the phase of development of Egyptian art, in which—to use the current terminology of art history—the period of the Ist Dynasty might be called 'archaic', the period of the IVth and Vth Dynasties 'classical', and the period of the XIIth Dynasty 'the first Renaissance'. The development of portraiture in these epochs depended on the different ways of linking elements of traditional stylisation, elements of racial character and those gained from observation of reality. The process ended with a brief period of realism, which, however, soon gave way before the advance of a new wave of idealisation.

The culminating period of the art of the Middle Kingdom lasted only a short time. It was limited, in fact, to the lifetimes of the last two rulers, Sesostris III and Amenemhet III. A rapid deterioration followed—the result of the confusion and uncertainty of the second critical

After the XXth Dynasty, art steadily declined until the time of the Ethiopian monarchs, when a new school arose, which emancipated itself from the slavish imitations and, by diligent study of the art of portrait-making and by a valiant effort, succeeded in producing masterpieces such as the statue of Mentumhet, who was governor of Upper Egypt under Taharka of Ethiopia. The same school, but perhaps several hundred years later, produced the portraits of bald-headed priests, in which the characteristic points (such as the shape of the skull) are indicated in a masterly manner, while the less significant details are ignored.

The photographs of the Forman brothers from the treasures of the Cairo Museum present to the general reader a brief but excellent idea of the art of Ancient Egypt as revealed in its funerary sculpture.

Moh. H. Abd-ur-Rahman

PREFACE

OVER A CENTURY AGO, IN 1858, THE DEPARTMENT OF ANTIQUITIES CAME into active being in Egypt. The antiquities gathered from excavations were first housed and exhibited in 1863 in a building in Boulac. In 1891, the collections, which had already reached an important number, were transferred to Giza. Finally, in 1902, they were moved to the building which they now occupy and which has become the wealthiest and most complete Egyptological Museum in the world.

The first signs of art in the Nile Valley appeared several centuries before the rise of the first pharaonic dynasties, about the year 3300 B. C. At the beginning of history, the sculptors worked anonymously in the royal workshops. The statues they carved were usually to be hidden away in special shrines or tomb chambers to ensure by magic means the immortality of the person represented. After a short development during the first two pharaonic dynasties, the climax was reached in the reign of Zoser, the founder of the IIIrd Dynasty, about 2800 B. C. The art of the statuary reached one of its highest points in the IVth and Vth Dynasties. In the statues of this period the chief stress is laid upon a faithful reproduction of the face; the rest of the body, especially the hands and feet, are conventionally treated.

After the first period of decay, the art of sculpture entered upon a new period of prosperity under the Middle Empire. Among its masterpieces were the fine statue of Amenemhet III and the statues and sphinxes of Tanis. These are marked by an emphatic rendering of the spiritual expression and are permeated by an appealing seriousness.

The comparatively numerous statues of the New Empire present a striking contrast to those of the Middle Kingdom. In place of the melancholy earnestness shown by the latter we find a certain placid and attractive cheerfulness. Examples worthy to rank with the best productions of the earlier period are not wanting. Among these may be mentioned the portrait head of Queen Nefertiti, the statue of the god Khonsu and the wooden bust of the time of Tutankhamen. In many cases artists have abandoned an attempt to produce a faithful portrait in favour of ideal beauty, devoting much of their energy to the presentation of the coiffure, the ornaments, and the flowing garments then fashionable. Many new types were invented in this period.

period in Egyptian history. This second period of decline reached its nadir with the invasion of the Hyksos, foreign rulers of Semitic origin who, settling in the Nile delta, easily conquered a large part of the disorganised kingdom. The Hyksos ruled over Egypt for almost a century, from 1680 to 1576 B. C. It was not until the middle of the sixteenth century that, under the leadership of the Theban princes, the founders of the XVIIth Dynasty, the greater part of the country was liberated. Egypt was not unified once again until King Ahmose I, founder of the XVIIIth Dynasty, conquered and laid waste Avaris, the capital of the Hyksos kings. For a long time thereafter his successors safeguarded the frontiers of Egypt against attack by Asiatic tribes by leading expeditions into Syria and Palestine.

The artists of the early XVIIIth Dynasty, strangely enough, took over the artistic traditions of the Middle Kingdom with far less hesitation than had once been the case with the artists of the XIth Dynasty, who, under similar circumstances, inherited the legacy of the Old Kingdom. The gap was in some ways easier to bridge because of the tendencies to idealisation of the sculpture of the period of Amenemhet III. The sculptors of the early XVIIIth Dynasty made use of all the forms from the period of Amenemhet: the seated and standing figures of kings, sanctified by recent tradition and from a formal point of view directly inspired by the statues of Sesostris III and Amenemhet III; the two types of royal sphinxes, the older with the royal head-dress and the younger, Amenemhet's, with the face framed by a lion's mane; figures of the king at sacrifice; and finally, in secular art, the block statue. This unbroken continuation from the culminating period of the Middle Kingdom was, however, only formal. The idealised depiction of reality reverted once again to stylised forms, with the artists again making use of ready-made formulae. Consequently, from the very beginning there was no convincing portraiture in the works of the XVIIth Dynasty, no attempt to depict character, such as we find in the portraits of Sesostris and Amenemhet. This powerful expressiveness had given the statues of the XIIth Dynasty monumentality even when they were of comparatively small size. The art of the XVIIIth Dynasty, on the contrary, was directed from the beginning into miniature forms, even in statues of colossal size. It had its basis in a certain gentle expression and in a new stylisation of the 'beautiful' form, which was, however, a reflection of real life. While the artists of the XIIth Dynasty had ceased to apply any trace of make-up to eyes and eyebrows (remember the eyes of Sesostris and Amenemhet) this idealising tendency soon gave way to the former manner, and the eyes assumed once again the 'beautiful' form—an elongated almond-shape, their outlines stressed by make-up, with the outer corners prolonged towards the temples and parallelled by the eyebrows. This manner of depicting eyes became the rule in relief and in free-standing sculpture right from the beginning of the XVIIIth Dynasty. Fashion caused certain changes, also, in real life, a trend towards enlarging the eyes by make-up and stressing their slanting position, not only in the case of women but also of men, as contemporary reliefs show. It is possible that the introduction of gentler forms in monumental sculpture was the result of the personal influence of Queen Hatshepsut. This highly energetic and gifted daughter of Thutmosis I, after a short marriage to her step-brother, Thutmosis II, ruled over Egypt as regent until her step-son, Thutmosis III, came of age. Even after this, she succeeded in reducing him to a mere background figure for a very long time. For twenty years she ruled unchallenged, concentrating during this period on the re-organisation of the state and the consolidation of conditions within the country. She fostered the arts and bequeathed to coming generations the famous terraced temple at Deir-el-Bahri. She encouraged all new and bold undertakings, and on her initiative a great expedition was sent to the legendary Land of Punt whence, from time immemorial, Egypt had imported perfumes and rare woods. She had the story of the expedition recorded for all time in a row of reliefs on the terraces of her temple (Plate 45).

However, the works of art of her reign did not endure. After her death Thutmosis III at last ascended the throne for which he had waited so long. He, too, came from a family of strong and energetic personalities and could not forgive his step-mother for having forced him into the insignificant role of successor. In revenge, he had most of her statues destroyed and her name removed from all monuments.

The queen's attitude to the question of her successor was very interesting and was reflected in the arts. Hatshepsut, who, after her mother, Queen Ahmose, was the real heiress to the kingdom since her father, Thutmosis I, was not of royal blood, ascended the throne not as a woman but as a true pharaoh, and always had herself depicted as such.

It was she who, possibly on the advice of her favourite architect, Senmut, chose models from the period of Amenemhet III for her statues. It may well have been that this ruler in his life served also as a model for the young queen, since his name long remained alive in Egyptian tales as a great king whose peaceful policies had brought well-being to the country.

The two types of sphinxes of the queen have survived, one with a head framed by a lion's mane (Plate 49). The statue of the seated queen is reminiscent of Amenemhet's limestone statue from Hawara with a quiet, cheerful expression. The queen's standing statue with the royal wig is, from the formal point of view, a copy of the statues of Amenemhet and Sesostris. It is rather touching to observe how, on the statues, the young girl's face tried to achieve the solemnity becoming in a ruler by calling to its aid every possible item of ceremonial attire, not excluding even the royal beard, which in the standing statue is far more striking than in the sphinx. The task of the artists who were entrusted with the fashioning of the queen's statues cannot have been without interest. Some of them only placed the gentle head of a queen on top of an idealised male figure, others, as, for instance, the maker of the statue of the seated queen in the Metropolitan Museum in New York, attacked the complicated problem with far greater honesty. The queen, dressed only in a kilt, has slim, delicate woman's arms and legs, small hands, and fine but faintly marked breasts. Her face with the tiny, vaguely pouting mouth, the pointed chin and the comparatively large aquiline nose recalls the family resemblance to Thutmosis III, whose father was Hatschepsut's step-brother. The eyes on all the queen's statues have a stylised shape with elongated outer corners.

The statues of Thutmosis in most cases show an even greater formal idealism than Hatshepsut's statues. He is probably most faithfully depicted in the larger than life-size statue of the king with the White Crown, today in the Cairo Museum; even here, however, the eyes and mouth have a stylised shape. Thutmosis III was a born warrior, and it is no wonder that the peaceful policy of his step-mother was a severe trial for his patience. He undertook a number of campaigns which resulted in his bringing Syria and Palestine under Egyptian rule. A number of his portraits, too, were based on models of the Amenemhet III period, such as the statue of Thutmosis offering sacrifice, of which, unfortunately, only the lower portion has survived (Plate 52). An obsidian head in the Cairo Museum has been thought to be Thutmosis (Plate 68). Although not all the statues of the king have such pregnantly expressive features as the portrait with the White Crown, all, at least superficially, maintain the line of the profile with the strikingly big nose, which is completely missing in the obsidian head.

Even the secular sculpture of the early New Kingdom period had its origins in the traditions of the XIIth Dynasty. We find seated figures wrapped tightly in cloaks, standing male figures in long kilts and, finally, block statues (Plate 50). Here, too, one is struck by the refinement of form. Small statues of women with slim figures and long, beautifully formed legs and noble features were frequent, and here and there among them an attempt at individualisation is evident (Plate 55).

This concentration on refined and dignified art-forms continued into the middle period of the XVIIIth Dynasty—known as the Golden Age—during the reigns of Amenhotep II, Thutmosis IV and Amenhotep III (whom the modern historians have called 'the Magnificent'). Thanks to the energetic campaigns of Amenhotep's predecessors, Egypt's power was firmly established during this period and appeared unshakeable. Her domination over distant lands brought with it many exotic innovations in the lives of the wealthy Egyptian upper classes. During this period of peace the everyday life of these classes grew more refined and sophisticated. This is perhaps most clearly shown in the art of the period. The simple Egyptian garment, the kilt, worn by men, and the ankle-length close-fitting dresses of the women, which were worn by both rich and poor as late as the early period of the New Kingdom, were suddenly replaced by soft, richly pleated garments. The toilet of the noble ladies was enriched by large, skilfully designed wigs held by diadems, with lotus flowers above the forehead. On the crown of the head was affixed a cone of fragrant unguent so that women literally moved in a cloud of perfume. The women's fashions were adopted even by some of the men. The wealth of jewels, necklaces, ear-rings and bracelets worn by both sexes hardly needs mention. In the carefully made-up faces shone artificially elongated and enlarged eyes under carefully painted brows. Life was beautiful and comfortable, spent in entertainments and feasts, at which musicians played and professional dancers performed. The men went hunting into the desert in light two-wheeled chariots, or in boats into the thick papyrus marshes full of wild fowl, which they brought down with arrows or boomerangs. Gone was the age of the virile warrior. The men of Amenhotep III's court were cultivated, refined, smooth courtiers, attending no less carefully to their appearance than their womenfolk. Their features are somewhat effeminate; not only their faces but even their bodies are softer and more rounded (Plate 66). Among the multitude of sweet 'beautiful' faces exceptions can be found from time to time. Notice the two statues of an important court official of that time, Amenhotep, son of Hapu (Plates 63 and 64). The first of these statues is a work of mannerist idealism whose sweet beauty derives strength from an almost melancholic concentration. The second is a real portrait, apparently intentionally archaic in style, which very consciously followed the traditions of the XIIth Dynasty.

Another example of the high standard achieved in portraiture is the small head of Queen Tiy carved in green basalt (Plate 53). The queen was yet another remarkable woman who sat on the Egyptian throne. She was not born of a noble family, as the names of her parents are given without titles. Amenemhet III clearly married a wife of his own choosing, and Tiy proved worthy of her position. She undoubtedly played a far more important role in the life of the court than that of the first wife in the king's harem; her influence on her husband was very great and lasting, and it seems that she had much to say in affairs of state. Her name appeared by the side of that of Amenhotep on numerous royal inscriptions. The basalt head is the face of the young Tiy who had barely left girlhood behind her. She is wearing a big ceremonial wig crowned by a diadem with two uraei; between them is a cartouche with the queen's name. The value of this portrait is enhanced by a comparison with the well-known ebony head of the queen in the Berlin Museum. In profile, the queen has the characteristic straight line of the nose, pouting lips with drooping corners, and a small, slightly receding chin. In full face the drooping line of the closed lips is even more striking, but it does not give the face an expression of bitter pessimism as in the portrait of Sesostris III; on the contrary, the effect is of slight, rather charming caprice. The somewhat slanting, narrow eyes have an idealised shape, but show no trace of make-up. All the features of the queen were reproduced much more distinctly by the maker of the ebony head. In fact, on comparing the two heads, J. C. Aldred came to the conclusion that, because of their general resemblance, the Berlin portrait was not of Queen Tiy but of her daughter, Sit-Amen, the probable mother of Tutankhamen (J.C. Aldred, *New Kingdom Art in Ancient Egypt*, p. 67, Tiranti, 1951). We are of the opinion that the small differences in the configuration of the lips, chin and eyes can well be explained by the fact that the ebony head represents the queen as a mature woman, perhaps even in old age, and that its conception is closer to the style of the early Tell-el-Amarna period, a typical mark of which was the often exaggerated stress on characteristic facial features. On comparing the little basalt head with the well-known relief depiction of Queen Tiy, we see that the differences are still greater, as the expressive line of the profile is largely suppressed on those reliefs.

32 The art of the period of Amenhotep II is an art of classically balanced forms, which were frequently repeated in finely differentiated variations during the period of mannerism. In this more-or-less unified stream of general development one occasionally comes across islands of realism, which, deviating from the taste of the period, probably reflected the new ideas that were beginning to penetrate that carefree and oversophisticated ruling class. One of the rebels against the sacred traditions was King Amenhotep III himself. How great an importance he attached to his personal life is shown by his selection as his wife and co-regent of a girl from a 'middle class' family. Nor did he ever try to justify his act by inventing a myth. On the contrary, he had the lowly origin of his wife publicly inscribed for all to admire as an object of his special pride. And he asserted his right of choice with unaccustomed determination. The longing for natural and free expression, at least in private matters and in emotional life, arose, undoubtedly, from a reaction to the traditions that had restricted the life of the mighty to formal ceremonies full of often incomprehensible symbolism.

In art there are occasional glimpses of a striving after a new realism in the circle closest to the royal court, for example, in the portraits of Queen Tiy, in some less official pictures of the king (e.g. the ebony statue in the Brooklyn Museum, in manner of execution so close to the little ebony head of the queen in the Berlin Museum that they might be considered the work of one artist) and some statues of high-ranking officials close to the king, as, for instance, the second statue of Amenhotep, son of Hapu.

Amenhotep III's almost ostentatious break with tradition was not merely personal. The cause was far more profound. The guardians of tradition whom the king was challenging were the priests of the Theban Temple of Amon, men made immensely wealthy by the loot and compulsory tribute of the Asiatic tribes whom Amenhotep's predecessors had conquered. The once insignificant god of the town had become, under the reign of the first kings of the XVIIIth Dynasty, the first god in the Egyptian state and had gradually become identified with other, formerly more important, gods until all had merged into the sun god, Re. The kings who had been occupied with the business of war probably had not had time to appreciate fully the growing power of the priests of the Amon-Re cult. At the time when Amenhotep's father, Thutmosis IV, ascended the throne, the High Priest of Amon was second only in power to the pharaoh himself. Thutmosis had already tried to curb this power, and his policy was continued even more vigorously by Amenhotep III, who realised that unless this development were checked the monarchy would become subordinate to the priesthood. The tension between the royal court and the Temple of Amon grew more and more acute, but during the reign of Amenhotep III the struggle was carried on by circumspect and indirect methods. The king stressed his own divine nature and gradually managed to deprive the High Priest of Amon of certain high offices. Simultaneously, he gave his support to those priests of the originally independent cult of the sun who had not become integrated with the cult of Amon.

This issue came to dominate the politics of the period from the time that Amenhotep created his son, Amenhotep IV (Akhenaton), his co-ruler. It is very probable that in view of the exceptional personalities of both parents, the education of the young prince did not follow traditional lines. Amenhotep III clearly made no secret of his views on the priesthood to his son, and from the very beginning of his co-rule Akhenaton proceeded to limit their power much more radically than had his father, basing his campaign on the support of the priests of the former cults of the sun. The struggle, which at first was purely political, was before long transferred to the sphere of ideas—this undoubtedly being Akhenaton's personal contribution. The young ruler had an exceptionally highly developed ability for independent theoretical thinking. Starting at the doctrines of the old cult of the sun he developed his own until he arrived at a picture of the Sun God freed from all the ancient myths. His god, called by one of the ancient names for the sun god, Harakhty Aton, was the fiery ball of the sun itself sending its life-giving rays to the earth. The king did not remain satisfied with a mere theoretical formulation of the new religion. His energy and his position gave him the power to put his ideas into practice.

The ideological struggle against the priests of Amon took on a new character with the introduction of definite political measures. The king, completely consistent in thought and deed, even changed his own name. Amenhotep, which meant 'Amon is satisfied', was clearly in conflict with the facts and did not correspond to the doctrine which the king proclaimed in such an uncompromising manner. He adopted a new name, Akhenaton, 'it pleases Aton' or 'beneficial Aton'. He decided to abolish the cult of Amon and to remove all the names of Amon from public inscriptions. At the same time the cults of other gods were prohibited, for Aton was henceforth to be the only god in Egypt. Finally, the young king left Thebes and founded a new town half-way between Thebes and Memphis, which he called Akhetaton, 'Aton's Horizon'. He transferred his court and administration there, and determined never to leave.

The foundation and construction of Akhetaton resulted in the creation of an enormous number of works of art which very faithfully reflect the ideas of the background from which they sprang.

It is interesting to examine how the new spirit made itself felt in Akhetaton (today called el-Amarna). The works of the earliest period show an unusually sharp reaction against the balanced classical, not to say mannerist, art of the period of Amenhotep III. They went, in fact, to the opposite extreme. Akhenaton's artists (undoubtedly at the wish of their master) rejected the 'beautiful' form and, instead, especially in relief, achieved a realism that might almost be called a caricature of reality, were it not obvious that it was meant absolutely seriously. It must not be forgotten, however, that the artists had already worked at the court of Akhenaton's father, and we may well imagine that to begin with they found the new style very difficult to master.

Akhenaton cannot have been a man of outstanding physique or physical beauty, but we can hardly imagine that he looked as he is depicted in the reliefs of the early Tell-el-Amarna period. He is shown with a shapeless head resting on a long thin neck, almost female breasts, a thin waist, a weak paunch overhanging powerful thighs that pass into stick-like shins. The figures of the queen and the princesses are only slightly more balanced. The artists in striving for the truth as demanded by the king concentrated on the negative aspects of his face and figure, and Akhenaton, as seen in Plate 70, was represented as a combination of all those negative elements. We see this style again in the colossal statue of the king at Karnak, where the picturesque conception of the strictly symmetrically worked face, with its sharply defined and exaggerated details, displays almost Secession features. The artists of the early el-Amarna period ruthlessly destroyed the 'beautiful' form and introduced new content under the influence of Akhenaton's religion. This found expression mainly on reliefs. In principle, however, the sculptors remained true to tradition. The depiction of the human figure in profile, even though the outline and proportions were deformed and unreal, is identical with the panels of, for instance, Hesire; the various mutual proportions of the figures on the reliefs, indicating their relative importance, also follow the old tradition, and even in the portrayals of children the artists in most cases did not go beyond depicting them as adults.

Tradition was, thus, not rejected so completely as might at first sight appear. From a formal point of view, too, the early el-Amarna period is far from what it is usually claimed to be, a period of healthy realism. On the contrary: it is mannerism turned inside out. When the initial wave of violent reaction receded, the development of the el-Amarna art turned in a different direction, and this still during the lifetime of Akhenaton. The real advance of the early el-Amarna art was in its subject matter, in the sense that the requirement of truthfulness opened the gate to a more intimate portrayal of human feelings, something which Egyptian art had hitherto avoided.

After a short initial period of experiment the el-Amarna artists began, without completely abandoning the requirements of realism, to seek new, more aesthetic, forms. Their search led them, via the distortions of 'super-realism', to a completely new mode of sculpture, one which relied on outline and used the effects of light and shade in composition.

In the long history of Egyptian art the el-Amarna period was but a short interval. The time of its most intense activity under Akhenaton lasted only twelve years. After the pharaoh's death work at el-Amarna continued for another three years, the period when the young king, Tutankhamen, and his wife, the third daughter of Akhenaton, were largely under the influence of Queen Nefertiti. Her death meant the end of Akhenaton and a return to Thebes; with this came the suppression of the heretical religion of Akhenaton and a return to the old cult of Amon. The works of art of the period survived only because no one took any interest in the deserted town. The shortness of the el-Amarna experiment makes it difficult to trace any definite line of development, even allowing for the great number of monuments that have survived. It may well be that what we call the early and the late stages existed side by side for a time as expressions of individual artists or schools. It is symptomatic that many of the surviving monuments are in an unfinished state—models or casts found in the workshop of the sculptor Thutmosis at el-

Amarna by the German expedition under the leadership of Borchardt; many of these have not even been identified.

Portraits of Akhenaton and even those of Nefertiti are fairly easy to identify, but those of the princes, princesses and young queens are not so easy. All the faces betray a certain family relationship so that it is difficult to distinguish between one or other of the known historical figures. The faces of the young princesses show an interesting mixture of the traits of both parents. All inherited their father's full mouth with its almost pathologically feverish expression, modelled in a dignified form that resembles the beautiful lips of their mother. The little head of the youngest girl carved in brown limestone (Berlin Museum) is like the father in facial expression, with its slightly protruding, somewhat asymmetrical chin. The features of the eldest daughter (Cairo Museum) are like those of the queen, particularly when viewed full face. But nobody knows, nor shall we ever know, which of the princesses is portrayed. Both heads have the strikingly elongated skulls typical of the early Tell-el-Amarna period. The face of the elder princess is no longer that of a child but of a young girl in adolescence or even maturity. In view of this and other stylistic features—refinement of form, absence of caricature in details and the peculiar summary modelling of the eyes (finished in colour)—we can attribute the work to the middle period.

The same is true of the unfinished head of Queen Nefertiti in the Cairo Museum (Plate 67) carved out of quartzite. It is a portrait of a very beautiful and mature woman whose charm is further enhanced by the el-Amarna style which took full account of the effects of light and shade. The eyes are modelled only on the upper lid, the edge of which throws a slight shadow over the slanting part of the eyes proper. The whole face reveals a certain tension, the result of the contrast between the definite lines of the beautiful mouth and the fine, superficially modelled parts of the face, forehead and chin. Quite probably the details of modelling were meant to have been completed in colour, in which case the face perhaps might have lost some of its attraction for us. Akhenaton's sudden and premature death meant that some works remained unfinished in the sculptor's workshop, hidden, as it were, under a final veil, which, especially in the face of the queen, added an almost unearthly charm to the flowering beauty cast forever in the stone.

The final stage of development of the el-Amarna period can be documented from the extremely rich inventory of the tomb of Tutankhamen, which gives us a complete picture of a luxuriously furnished royal household. A large number of everyday objects found in the tomb were clearly not made for that express purpose but must previously have filled a place in the chambers of the royal palace. The articles, as well as the sculptures and reliefs, are evidence of the astonishingly high level of Egyptian arts and crafts. The mask of Tutankhamen (Plate 71) is not merely a portrait of the young king who found his death prematurely, but primarily an outstanding example of the jewellers' skill, as are the reliefs on his second coffin (Plate 83). The skill of the Egyptian craftsmen in their various techniques and the perfection of their work never ceases to surprise.

As far as we can judge from the sculptures and reliefs in Tutankhamen's tomb and from several other works attributed to that period, the development of the late el-Amarna art followed the lines laid down during the middle period. It is possible that our opinion on the middle period is influenced by the unfinished objects in the workshop of Thutmosis, the mysterious beauty of which make an impression on us even in their incomplete state. It seems, though, that the art of the Tutankhamen period aimed at more clearly defined shapes and a more precise elaboration of detail. The return to the cult of Amon meant, in the sphere of the arts, a return to the traditional stylised forms, the eyes with the artificially elongated outer corners and the eyebrows. It is interesting to compare the mask of Tutankhamen, his depiction on the coffins and the faces of his statues found in the tomb.

The stylised form of the eyes is the same everywhere, and is even identical with the eyes on some of the animal sculptures found in the tomb. The relief scenes retained that warm and intimate charm which is typical of the scenes of family life under Akhenaton. One of them, depicting the young king and queen in ceremonial court dress with rich crowns, decorates the back-rest of Tutankhamen's throne. It looks as though, quite without regard for the court ceremonial, they are talking informally to each other. Perhaps even more charming is a scene, wrought in beaten gold, depicting duck shooting. The young queen, still wearing a child's lock, is handing her husband an arrow. With her left hand she is pointing to a papyrus thicket where frightened ducklings are cackling in their nest. We do not know what the artist was trying to express with that gesture; perhaps it was added merely for compositional reasons, or perhaps the young queen felt sorry for the ducklings and wished to draw her husband's attention to them to prevent his shooting them: who can tell? We shall never be able to detect all the fine nuances in the subject matter of these scenes.

Even in the monumental art of the late XVIIIth Dynasty certain features of the younger members of Akhenaton's family reappear. The full mouths with the beautifully cut lips in the faces of the god Khonsu (Plates 72 and 73) and the god Amon (Plate 80) recall the face of Tutankhamen and his elder brother, Smenkh-ka-ra. The colossal quartzite statue (Plate 77) is reminiscent of the plaster masks of Akhenaton in the expression of the mouth. The charming little face of the young queen, with the tiara carved in wood and covered with a layer of gesso and pigment (Plate 76), is related to the faces of the statuettes found in Tutankhamen's tomb. Here, the detailed drawing of the eyes has the same lines as are found in the four busts of the king on the lids of his funerary vessels. It is more than likely that it is a portrait of Tutankhamen's wife, Princess Ankhes-en-amon.

In the shadow of that magnificent court there continued to exist, as in the period of the Old and the Middle Kingdoms, the art of the private tombs. Although this was more modest, in most cases, in its use of precious metals, and the workmanship was less painstaking than that of the royal tombs, yet in its main features it was influenced by the fashion set by the court. This can be seen very clearly in the reliefs depicting Ptah-May and his wife Tiy (Plate 75), which are distant variations on the el-Amarna theme. They link conservative elements—the faces of husband and wife recall the 'beautiful' style of the period of Amenhotep III—with formal elements taken from el-Amarna. The latter can be detected in the outlines of the figures and in the characteristically relaxed muscles of the lower part of the body. At el-Amarna was found the wooden statuette of the Lady Res (Plate 92) whose lips clearly resemble the pouting lips in the portrait of Queen Tiy.

It has already been pointed out that Akhenaton's reforms enriched Egyptian art from the point of view of subject matter by opening the way to the expression of emotion, which up to that time had been avoided. The el-Amarna reliefs chiefly depict scenes of happy family life, but include also a relief in which the royal parents mourn the death of their little daughter, Maketaton. In the tomb reliefs of the late XVIIIth Dynasty we can notice two contradictory approaches. On the one hand, we find reliefs in the old tradition, showing the deceased sitting quietly in front of the table of offerings, and on the other, there are reliefs where room was found for emotion and the expression of the feeling of bereavement. Into the stone were engraved funeral processions with groups of wildly lamenting women, for example those in Plate 84. Emotions and passions were expressed by the artists in the gestures of the hands and also—and here was truly something new in Egyptian art—in the expressions on the contorted faces. These moving funeral scenes reappear in various forms throughout the XIXth Dynasty.

As an example, let us take the scene of dancers at such a funeral, with the men walking in rows of two and three and a tightly packed group of women beating drums (Plate 93). Here, the sculptor has even tried to suggest a second plane in the picture by depicting only the upper part of the bodies of the women in the second row. The artist who carved the funeral procession of men (Plate 95) really succeeded in solving the problem of perspective. The heads of the men as they walk side by side in rows of three and four grow smaller as they recede into the background and are carved in such a way that the tops of the heads form a horizontal line while the chins make an ascending line. From the point of view of perspective this sketchy relief is quite exceptional and deserves careful attention. Compare it with the relief of the funerary dance (Plate 93) where the heads of the rows of three men are the same size and the attempt at depicting a second row of dancing girls is rather clumsy. However, the consistent use of perspective as in Plate 95 in reliefs of this nature is an exceptional event in Egyptian art generally, although it does go some way towards refuting the older view which did not concede the existence of any expression of depth in Egyptian art.

After the return of the court from Akhetaton to Thebes the artists quietly reverted to the old formal tradition, which they could hardly have had time to forget during the brief el-Amarna interlude. It is therefore easy to understand how the artists at the end of the XVIIIth and the beginning of the XIXth Dynasties continued to use the 'beautiful' mannerist style of the period of Amenhotep III. The art of the el-Amarna period had very little subsequent influence, both because of the shortness of its flowering and because Akhenaton was considered to be a heretic. The colossal alabaster statue thought to be of Seti I (Plate 88) still retains certain facial characteristics of the late el-Amarna period, although its execution is smoother and more schematic. While, superficially, the artists of the late XVIIIth and the early XIXth Dynasties went in for much subtle detail in their portraits, as may be seen in the statue of Khet-min and his wife (Plates 46, 47, 51), or in the magnificent limestone torso of the king (Plate 100), true individuality and expressiveness receded into the background, especially in monumental sculpture. The portraits of Ramses II are chiefly remarkable for an indifferent gracious smile, the only truly individual feature being the fairly large, bent nose. This condescending and impersonal smile which frequently appeared in the official sculptures of Amenemhet III, was perfected technically by a dent along the raised corners of the mouth (Plate 91). The pharaoh's smile with its refined, rather girlish and dreamy expression reappears on the face of the princess in Plate 96. But we should not forget that the graciously smiling kings of the early XIXth Dynasty were far from being the effeminate, refined courtiers that some of their portraits might suggest. Seti I and Ramses I, though the life at their court was luxurious, were energetic warriors whose aim was to renew the prestige and power of Egypt, which had sunk so low under the heretic pharaoh, Akhenaton. Their indefatigable campaigns helped to restore Egypt's domination over Syria and Palestine and saved the Great Egyptian Empire of Thutmosis II, though not to its full extent. Both pharaohs were great builders and had their own deeds glorified in reliefs and inscriptions which decorated the walls of their temples. Elaborate battle scenes were very popular, in which the king in his chariot, drawn by two rearing fiery horses, was the central motif. Before him crouched the routed and terror-stricken enemy. The subject matter is identical with that of the painted casket in Tutankhamen's tomb (Plate 69), the only difference being that the artist who depicted the battle scenes of the kings of the XIXth Dynasty could have drawn his subject matter from real life.

The relief of the king holding a group of his defeated enemies by the hair (Plate 85) tells the same story as Narmer's palette at the beginning of Egyptian history. There is very little difference in execution and content, even though the later work differed in form.

Egyptian art during the period of the XIXth Dynasty was the swan song of a great epoch which had reached its peak in the elegant mannerism of the reign of Amenhotep III and the remarkable experiment of the el-Amarna period. But although an epilogue, it had much to say. The first kings of the Dynasty succeeded in restoring the might of Egypt and created a background of luxury to court and upper class life, largely as the result of the loot of conquered territories. All this found expression during the period of Ramses II in enormous constructional works. The source of creative invention, however, was gradually drying up. It is easy to understand that the mannerism of official art should frown upon any other styles but its own, which more and more refinement of detail and the urge towards perfectionism were gradually drying up and killing. The monumental reliefs of battle scenes fared little better. Only the cursory carvings of funeral scenes in the private tombs retained some of the feeling of rapture which had characterised the el-Amarna period.

The first kings of the XIXth Dynasty succeeded in holding the empire together for a short period, but after the death of Ramses II uprisings broke out in the Asian colonies. On the other side Egypt was threatened by Libyan invasions into the Nile delta. The great empire, which up to that time had quietly enjoyed the fruits of its conquests, suddenly found itself on the defensive; and from then on this was to be permanent. The second king of the XIXth Dynasty, Ramses III, managed to ward off the danger for a time by skilful defensive campaigns. He was succeeded by a number of weaker kings of the same name, under whose rule the internal organisation of the country completely disintegrated. The last Ramses of the XXth Dynasty was succeeded by the High Priest of Amon, Hrihor. At last the priests' hour had come. But it was too late, for it came at a time when Egyptian power had lost all significance.

After the dynasty of the priests followed a dynasty of Libyan origin; then even the princes of Nubia ruled over proud Egypt. In the seventh century B. C. the energetic kings of the XXVIth, the Saite, Dynasty managed to unify the dismembered empire once again, and even tried to reconquer the colonies in Asia Minor. Here, however, Egypt collided with the Babylonian empire, and the struggle ended in a heavy defeat of the Egyptian army at Carchemish in 605 B. C. The defeat in Asia did not greatly affect conditions inside the country, where the upper classes continued to live in peace and luxury. The penultimate king of the Saite Dynasty, Ahmose, even managed to conquer the island of Cyprus. Soon after Ahmose's death in 525 B. C. following her defeat at the Battle of Pelusium, Egypt succumbed to the Persian King Cambyses. Artists continued to draw inspiration from the enormous heritage accumulated throughout the ages. Sharing the fate of the Egyptian empire they yet showed more resistance. Even during the darkest days of the Empire when no large-scale building requiring the brilliance of sculptured and painted decorations was being undertaken, there remained plenty of work. People still died firmly believing in the eternal kingdom of Osiris, and who else but the artists could help to see their faith was not disappointed? The sculptors, according to their abilities and the opportunities open to them, continued to carve reliefs on the walls of tombs, sometimes carefully, quite often sketchily or carelessly (Plates 107, 115). They made stelae, statues and statuettes of the deceased and *shabti* figures, also depicting the deceased, which were to carry out all the work for him in the tomb. The painters decorated the coffins and ilustrated the scrolls which contained all that awaited the deceased in the Underworld, all the questions that he might resent and the answers to them, to help him reach the palace of Osiriș without blemish. The illustrations on these scrolls show that the artists of the late period of the New Kingdom were skilful craftsmen with a feeling for sensitive, pure and fresh line, and for effective composition of scenes, sometimes drawn from daily life, sometimes depicting strange, awe-inspiring events in the Underworld (Plates 106, 114, 116).

The sculpture of the late period is plainly eclectic. The artists did not follow tradition in a natural manner, as handed down in the workshops from master to disciple, but consciously selected patterns from the past. Some works of the late period show a love of antiquity which manifested itself not only in copies of the garments and postures of the Old Kingdom statues but also in attempts to reproduce their scale of proportions. Sometimes in the course of such work the artist would forget his original intention and complete his pseudo-archaic statue with a necklace in relief (cf. the statue of Harmakhis in Plate 104). Again, he would create an anachronistic mixture of ancient kilt and a New Kingdom fashion in royal head-dress or wig (cf. the statuette of King Osorkon III, Plate 108).

Side by side with the archaic style, which even depicted kings of foreign, barbarian origin as native Egyptians, at times lending them the solemn and dignified expressions of the kings of the earlier dynasties or, at others, the subtle charm of the kings of the New Kingdom, there existed in Egypt a second stream, which, as it were, reflected the best traditions of realism of the XIIth Dynasty. These statues possess an amazing rough grandeur of expression, as shown on the head of Mentuhotep (Plate 117) which reveals in its gross features the mixture of foreign, barbarian blood. Others, by contrast, display a weary, smooth-featured refinement, such as the famous 'Green Head' in Berlin, which is not only a portrait of an elderly individual but the apotheosis of the old age of a nation.

Once again, during the period of the Saite Dynasty, the skilful policies of several capable kings succeeded in bringing unity to the country, and for a time Egypt experienced a flowering not unlike the culminating periods of the New and Middle Kingdoms. The reorganisation of the state left its mark also on the arts, though it was unable to give them new inner strength and creative invention. An intensive building programme was undertaken and monumental statues of the gods and the Saite pharaohs were created; but the work remained eclectic, based on models selected from the past. The works of this period are outstanding for their virtuosity in the handling of materials and the perfection of their finish, but they lack the spiritual content of the works of the great epochs. What is usually called the 'Saite Renaissance' was in fact an expression of eclecticism, a dry classicism which adopted the heritage of the past merely in its outward forms.

With the invasion of Alexander the Great, Egypt was absorbed into the Hellenistic world. The ancient dying culture met another which, although its greatest things were in the past, was still strong and flourishing. Egypt became the domain of foreign rulers who ordered its affairs according to their own ways; Egyptians ceased to be masters in their own country for thousands of years. Egyptian art put up an opposition to Hellenism with a sullen stubbornness worthy of its great past. As long as the belief in the eternal life of Osiris continued, Egyptian art fought for its right to independent existence. It lost it only when the new religion uprooted its very basis.

Even today, Egyptian art remains for many an art shrouded in a veil of exotic mystery which is difficult to penetrate. Some scholars, even, have chosen to emphasise the complex and mysterious laws of composition in reliefs and statues, which, in their view, were known only to the initiated among the priests. But the content of the art is not changed by complexity of construction. Today, with a little effort and the use of geometrical analysis, these difficulties can soon be overcome. It is the content that makes Egyptian art the simplest and most vital evidence that any nation has left of its own past. The Egyptians did not wish to be mysterious. What they left on the walls of the tombs they tried to relate as comprehensibly as possible, using every means they knew and even engraving explanatory notes in hieroglyphics when they wished to leave no doubt as to their meaning. But they could hardly foresee that their work would speak to generations so far in the future. It did not concern them that their work would be seen only with the eyes of eternity. In their naive realism they were truthful, even when their stories were grossly exaggerated, like those of children with a bold imagination. In the Old Kingdom their kings were the embodiment of their gods, and they depicted them accordingly, with expressions of solemn majesty corresponding to their ideal. Their high officials, though dignified personages, were, however, human beings, and the artists gave them their due in trying to set upon their faces the stamp of real life. The rulers of the Middle Kingdom were still the embodiment of the gods; but at the same time they were energetic rulers of their country, generals and masters, and in spite of the myth about their divine origin they had to fight hard for their position. The Egyptian artists understood and depicted even these nuances. The later kings of the XIIth Dynasty, as preserved for us by the sculptors, were first of all imposing personalities, who through their work and their appearance, left a profound and lasting impression upon the spirit of the nation.

No less truthful were the artists of the New Kingdom. They were no good at pretence. However hard the artists carving the statue of Hatshepsut tried to conceal the woman within, the mask lacked conviction. The highly groomed figures of the kings and officials of the late XVIIIth Dynasty bear witness to the life of the time. If Akhenaton had not encouraged his artists to depict their environment we should know far less about his religious ideas than we in fact do. And this applied everywhere. Egyptian art fought for its existence until the abandonment of the belief in the Kingdom of the Great Osiris tolled its death-knell.

It has often been said that Egyptian art was so anonymous and tied down by tradition that it had very little room left for even a slow development. But were there not other great periods in art that were equally bound by tradition and equally anonymous without our condemning them on that score? What, for instance, do we know about the Master of Naumburg cathedral? No more than about the sculptor who once, long ago, carved the head of Queen Nefertiti. Development, it is true, was slow, but then Egyptian art developed from its own roots without foreign influences; nor was it in a position to borrow anything from outside its own tradition that might have stimulated its advance. The bonds of tradition were indeed strong and yet the Egyptian artist developed an enormous scale of nuances in form and subject matter, ranging from the solemn and monumental to the humorous.

Unknown workers, who will forever remain unknown, engaged on decorating the walls in the tombs of the mighty of their world, the artists left records of themselves, their work and that of their fellow workers in other crafts, records of their daily life and all its trivial and amusing episodes. The only thing they did not care to relate were sad stories. On the walls of temples they unfolded enormous battle scenes from the campaigns of their kings in the way they imagined heroic deeds to be, just as in a fairy story. In tiny illustrations on the scrolls of the Books of the Dead they revealed their beliefs and their fears. No other nation ever revealed more of itself in its art than the Egyptians, and none spoke so openly and so truthfully. Thanks to this undisguised truthfulness with which, more than three thousand years ago, they related the story of the life of a nation, Egyptian art has remained a heritage of rare value, and one that amply repays any effort on our part to understand fully.

1—3, 6—7. RELIEF PANELS OF THE TOMB OF HESIRE

Wood. Average height 1.15 m. IIIrd Dynasty.

These are four of eleven wooden panels which once filled the niches in the unburnt brick walls of the mastaba of Hesire at Sakkara, where they were discovered by the French archaeologist Mariette. They were dated to the beginning of the IIIrd Dynasty on the basis of the seal cylinders of King Zoser, found in the same mastaba. The degree of preservation of the panels varies. In many cases the lower sections are badly damaged.

1. One of the best preserved panels. Hesire is depicted in a striding pose with the left foot forward. He is clad in ceremonial garments, consisting of a long wig and a kilt held by a belt. The sceptre he holds in his right hand and the tall crook in his left are insignia of authority, while the scribe's tools (also in the left hand) indicate his profession.

2. Another well-preserved panel. Hesire, wrapped in close-fitting robes tied over the left shoulder, is sitting in front of a little table with offerings (loaves of bread). In his left hand he holds against his breast a tall crook and a sceptre; the scribe's tools are thrown over his left shoulder. The bare right hand is reaching towards the table.

3. Detail of panel 2.

6. This panel has suffered considerable damage in the lower section. Hesire's pose and garments are identical with those shown on Plate 1, but his head is covered with a wig of tiny, tightly twisted curls. His right hand holds a tall crook close to his breast, and the scribe's tools are again thrown over his right shoulder. As a result of the damage it is impossible to determine whether or not he held a sceptre in his right hand.

7. Detail of another panel, again badly damaged. Hesire is clad in identical robes but wears a different wig.

In content and composition all these panels are variations on one theme. The deceased is depicted either standing or sitting, with all the symbols of his office, in this case in front of a table with offerings. The manner of portrayal, with the head in profile, the shoulders *en face*, the body twisted from the hips upwards in three-quarter profile and the legs again in pure profile, is characteristic of Egyptian art and remained the model for later periods.

Typical of the early period are such details as the depiction of two left legs, i.e. both legs shown with the big toes outward (similarly, the outstretched right hand in Plate 2 is shown as a left one). Outstanding, although not repeated in later periods, is the accomplished modelling of the naked parts of the body (especially in Plate 1), with its clearly marked clavicles, trunk muscles, arms and legs. The artist has even managed to convey an impression of effort in the muscles of the right arm holding the sceptre.

Especially noteworthy is the realistically and carefully carved left hand with which Hesire is holding the crook and the scribe's tools. The clenched fist clearly presented a lesser problem to the artist than the depiction of an open hand.

Finally, it should be noted that Hesire's profile is identical on all the panels, with differences only in the degree of finish of the face.

4—5. PRINCE RAHOTEP AND HIS WIFE NEFERT

Painted limestone. Height 1.20 m. Early IVth Dynasty.

Both statues were found in one mastaba near the pyramid of King Snefru at Meidum. Although each was carved separately, they should be considered as a double statue of husband and wife, a genre that was common in Egyptian art.

Prince Rahotep was the son of a king. He held the office of Commander-in-Chief of the royal army and other high ranks. Princess Nefert was also descended of royal blood. They are both sitting on seats of simple block shape. The artist used the empty space on the backs of the tall seats on both sides of their heads for inscriptions. The pose of the two figures is stiff, their bodies following the angle of the seat. All the life of the two statues is concentrated in the faces; the artist portrayed them as true to racial type rather than created real likenesses. This racial character is evident mainly in the shape of the mouth with its full lips and blunt corners. The eyes are stylised, but an extremely lifelike impression is achieved by inlaying the eyeballs with stones to resemble the colour and transparency of the human eye—the whites in milk-white flint, the pupils in crystal.

Rahotep's face gains a somewhat forced individuality from the wrinkles between the eyebrows. The artist achieved a more effective portrayal of a real person by the application of colour (black hair, light-tan skin for Rahotep and a more yellowy tinge for Nefert with white garments) and by touching in details of the faces and garments in paint.

8. GEESE FEEDING

Gesso and paint. Height of strip 0.27 m. Late IIIrd or Early IVth Dynasty.

This painting was taken from a wall in the mastaba of Nefermaat at Meidum. The section reproduced here shows the left half of the strip. The completely truthful delineation of the birds in this characteristic profile view shows the extraordinarily keen power of observation of the Egyptian artists. This may be seen, for instance, in the detail of the tiny teeth in the open beaks of the feeding geese and in the curve of their necks and crops. The profile depiction of walking geese, as seen in the right half of the picture is, of course, in simplified form, identical with the hieroglyphic symbol.

9. LIMESTONE SARCOPHAGUS

Height 0.10 m.

Giza. IVth Dynasty.

The shape of a house was common for sarcophagi of the Old Kingdom. The division of the walls indicates in stylised and simplified form the division of the walls of a real Egyptian house, and the constructional elements of a wooden building were faithfully transposed into stone. In contrast to sarcophagi carved out of granite, one example is all the more interesting for having its walls adorned with coloured ornaments, which include several characteristic motifs of the early period, taken over partly from mats and textiles.

10—11. STATUE OF KING KHAFRE (CHEFREN)

Black, white and yellow grained diorite. Height 1.68 m.

IVth Dynasty.

This statue was found in 1858 in the well by the entrance gate to the funerary temple of the Khafre pyramid. It is a typical example of the royal official portrait as it evolved during the IIIrd and early IVth Dynasties. The king is sitting on a throne in a stiff and majestic pose with the left palm flat on his left leg and the clenched right fist grasping the sash. He is wearing a ceremonial apron, his head is covered with a royal wig-cover with a uraeus-snake, and he has a ceremonial pharaonic beard.

The throne has a tall back-rest with sides in the form of stylised bodies of lions, between whose front and back paws is a symmetrically composed motif in relief of clusters of lotus and papyrus stalks symbolising the union of Upper and Lower Egypt. A sacred falcon sits on the back-rest of the throne—an embodiment of the god Horus, whose outspread wings envelop the king's head. The king's face, for all the simplification and summary modelling, retains certain aspects of portraiture, as seen, for example, in the broad expressive nose. This same feature in less noble form can be found in a small alabaster statue of the ruler (also in the Cairo Museum).

12—14. FALSE DOOR TO THE TOMB OF EIKA

Acacia wood. Height 1.93 m. Width 1.47 m. Height of Figure 0.73 m.

Late IVth or early Vth Dynasty.

The door was found not far from the road to the pyramid of King Venis. The construction of the door is identical with that of the present door. The individual parts are joined by strips of leather. The sections at the bottom and along the sides bear hieroglyphic inscriptions. The space between is filled in with relief scenes showing the dead man and his wife at a table with offerings. The flat parts surrounding the rectangular niche bear relief figures of Eika and his son (left side) and his wife and daughter (right side). The deceased is depicted in the same manner as Hesire (Plates 1 and 6), but the technique is different. The reliefs on the doors to Eika's tomb are worked in intaglio and the details and modelling of the body follow a much more schematic and conventional form; the canon of proportions, too, is far less harmonious. The little figure of the son is a tiny duplicate of the father. The figure of Eika's wife on the opposite side is equally conventional. She is dressed in a long, close-fitting garment, with a wig on her head, and wears a necklace and bracelets. In her raised right hand she is holding a lotus flower. The left hand is drawn inversely, i.e. as a right one. The little daughter is again a miniature version of the mother.

By the side of the Hesire reliefs, which are outstanding masterpieces, the Eika reliefs give one an idea of good, conventional craftsmanship.

15—17. JOY AND PEACE

Painted limestone reliefs. Height of figures 0.53 m. Early Vth Dynasty.

The reliefs originally came from the funerary temple of the pyramid of King Sahure at Abusir, not far from Sakkara. The figures reproduced here form part of a procession of gods bearing the pharaonic sacrifices. They represent the goddesses of Joy and Peace. Both the figures are carved in bas-relief. The goddesses are dressed in short, close-fitting garments tied over the right shoulder. They wear long wigs with straight strands of hair. In the right hand each holds a sceptre, and the forearms are adorned with the three symbols of life—*'nch*. They carry mats with bread, the hieroglyphic for *htp* (satisfied). The sculptor omitted the left hands, probably for reasons of composition. On the whole, the lay-out is ornamental, with a paratactical arrangement of motifs of equal significance.

18. SACRIFICE BEARERS

Painted limestone relief. Height of section 0.25 m. Vth Dynasty.

Part of a relief from the walls of the tomb of Nenkheftikai depicting a procession of men bearing offerings of gifts. The figures are shown in a typical manner, arranged in ornamental, paratactical order.

19—20. KA-APER called the SHEIK EL-BELED

Light brown wood (originally overlaid with gesso and painted). Height 1.10 m. Early Vth Dynasty.

This statue was found by the French archaeologist Mariette in a mastaba which, in his view, probably dated back to the IVth rather than the Vth Dynasty. The usual name, the Sheik el-Beled, was given to Mariette's statue by the workmen, whom it reminded of the headman of a neighbouring village.

Ka-aper is depicted in a posture reminiscent of the reliefs on Hesire's panels and on the Eika door. In the left hand he holds a tall staff (restored); the clenched right fist undoubtedly held a sceptre as a further symbol of authority. The left leg is striding forward. The garments are different in so far as the kilt is plain and falls to below the knee; the head is smooth-shaven. The statue is a masterpiece, displaying the corpulent dignity of Ka-aper by means of a convincing simplification of rounded forms, with stress laid on certain elements of portraiture, which here stand out more strongly than the stylised features. Note the faintly aquiline nose with its broad open nostrils, the soft line of the down-drawn mouth and the fine modelling of the puffy cheeks and double-chin. The one stylised feature in the face is the eyes. The lack of individual expression is compensated for, as in the statues of Rahotep and Nefert, by the application of coloured materials to the eyes—milk-white quartz for the whites, crystal for the iris and probably ebony for the pupils—to give an impression of vigour and alertness.

21. SEATED SCRIBE

White limestone. Traces of gesso and pigment. Height 0.51 m. Found in 1893 at Sakkara. Vth Dynasty.

Statue of an unknown scribe sitting in the characteristic position, tailor-fashion, with an open scroll of papyrus on his knees. The composition of the statue is determined by the three sides of a pyramid. The face is a mixture of stylisation and individual features. The modelling of the round cheeks is superficial; the stylisation of the eyes is lessened by their slanting position, with drooping outer corners. The sharp marking of the furrow along the nose gives the round face an unusual expression, which is further intensified by the light, barely noticeable drooping of the corners of the mouth. There is more than a touch of contempt mingled with the scribe's polite attentiveness as he waits for the dictated words.

22. SEATED SCRIBE

Mottled grey granite. Height 0.475 m. Found at Sakkara. Vth Dynasty.

The typical pose is here determined by the composition based on the shape of a three-sided pyramid. The sculptor has even gone so far as to adjust the proportions of the scribe's body to suit his end. The shins, for example, are almost as long as the body and head. In the frontal view the principle of axial symmetry is strictly adhered to. These almost abstract principles of construction contrast sharply with the realism of the modelling of the upper part of the body and certain parts of the face—the thick-set nose, the soft mouth and the unconventional shape of the eyes.

23. WOMAN WITH A LOTUS FLOWER

Painted limestone stele. Height of figure 0.36 m. Sakkara. Vth Dynasty.

Detail from the stele of the Lady Ihat, the wife of Nekawre, and her family. The Lady Ihat is depicted in the same way as the wife of Eika on the false door (Plates 13 and 14). The dead woman's small son, Sekhemka, is likewise depicted as a miniature figure of an adult with a child's lock. Conventional work of average level.

24. HEAD OF KING VESERKAF

Fragment of a colossal statue. Red granite. Height 0.67 m. Found near Veserkaf's pyramid at Sakkara. Vth Dynasty.

The head is an example of monumental sculpture in which stylisation predominates. The face is modelled in an overall manner with almost unnoticeable transitions; the eyes have the 'beautiful shape' with the outer corners and the line of the brows extended towards the temples. The mouth with its sharply defined lips shows a certain degree of stylisation. Typical of the ruler, perhaps, were the big shapeless nose and the weak chin. (Viewed from above in this reproduction, this latter feature appears less marked than it in fact is.)

25. Detail of the FALSE DOOR TO THE TOMB OF KA-EM-HESET

Wood. Height of figures 0.95 m. Vth Dynasty.

Ka-em-Heset, the building overseer, is depicted here in a traditional manner. His head is covered with a wig of tiny curls; he has a short, angular beard and wears a big heavy necklace around his neck. The most striking features are the almond-shaped eyes with their elongated outer corners and the stylised line of the long eyebrows. The work is in intaglio relief in which the visible parts of the body and face appear only in outline, while the surface remains unshaped and, apart from certain graphic details, almost without modelling.

26. MAN WITH BABOONS

Fragment of a painted limestone relief. Width 1 m. Found at Sakkara. Vth Dynasty.

The central motif of this fragment from a larger strip is the figure of a man leading two baboons on a leash. The female baboon bears her young; the male is catching another man, who is defending himself, by the leg. The scene is part of a procession of men bearing offerings to the deceased. Its monotonous, majestic rhythm is enlivened by this rather unusual detail in which the sculptor captured an occurrence in real life.

27. MUSICIANS AT A FEAST

Painted limestone relief. Average height of figures 0.18 m. Vth Dynasty.

Part of the relief decorating the walls of the tomb of Nenkheftikai at Sakkara, depicting a group of musicians accompanying a group of singers with harp, flute and long pipe. In contrast to the prevailing convention, several sitting figures are depicted here in full profile. The sculptor seems to have become so absorbed in the problem of the precise representation of the position of the hands and fingers of the musicians that he laid aside convention. This is especially so in the case of the harp and flute players. The full profile of the singers is also given, probably for compositional reasons. The lower strip of relief, of which we can only see part of the inscription, depicts a row of dancing girls.

28. THE GOD OF THE SEA

Painted limestone relief. Height of figures 0.53 m. Early Vth Dynasty.

Another detail of the relief of the procession of gods from the funerary temple of King Sahure at Abusir. Behind the figures of the goddesses of Joy and Pleasure (see Plates 15 and 17) walks the God of the Sea. The Egyptians depicted him, like the God of the Nile, as a half-male, half-female figure. The wavy, two-coloured lines that cover his body represent water and are identical with the hieroglyphic symbol for the Egyptian word *mv*—water. As in the case of the goddesses, the sculptor here has omitted the left hand. (It is of interest to note that in another relief in Sahure's temple with an identical motif the artist did not take this liberty.)

29. HEAD OF A WOMAN

Wood. Height 0.85 m. Found at El-Lisht neat the pyramid of King Sesostris I. Early XIIth Dynasty.

This small, unusual sculpture is normally dated to the early XIIth dynasty, according to the place where it was found. In view of its exceptional features it is difficult to say whether this ascription is correct.

The face is finely modelled, and the area round the mouth, in particular, is strongly expressive. Through the gentle but noticeable curve of the closed lips and the slight, asymmetrical upward slant at the corners, the Egyptian artist has managed to achieve a strange, mysterious half-smile that reminds one of the faces of women painted by Leonardo da Vinci. The impression is strengthened by the exceptionally large and elongated eyes (made from a different material and long since vanished or stolen) and the finely modelled line of the brows. The face is framed by a black wig made of painted wood inlaid with tiny gold squares. Their regular arrangement reveals that this was intended to represent a net of precious gold rather than individual ornaments of the hair.

30—31. STATUE OF A MAN

Wood. Height 1.08 m. Sakkara. VIth Dynasty.

Figure of a man in the accepted iconographic tradition with the left foot forward and the left arm close to the body. An example of average work of a good standard. On the surface, remnants of gesso and pigment have survived. The body is, on the whole, fashioned in a superficial manner; only the face shows certain individual features around the mouth (particularly the modelling of the mouth and chin) while the parts around the eyes are completely stylised.

32. THE FIGHTING BOATMEN

Painted limestone relief. Height 0.40 m. Width 1.40 m. Sakkara. VIth Dynasty.

The lower strip of the relief, which has survived almost intact, depicts a fight between boatmen. The scene is unusually lively, and the artist has placed within the compositional framework of three paratactically arranged boats groups of men fighting in a great variety of postures. Some of the boatmen are attacking each other with long poles, others are wrestling or falling into the water. This situation provided a splendid opportunity for the expression of body movement, even while keeping to the basic type of human figure. However, the artist did not hesitate to break the rules where he saw fit, and depicted some of the men in full profile. Especially interesting is the group in the boat at the right. Here, two men have come to blows and a third is holding the leg of another who has fallen into the water, while a fifth pokes him with the end of his pole. Shouts of encouragement (in the hieroglyphic inscription) accompany the battle: Hit him over the head! Break his back! and so on. The surface of the water is not indicated by a wavy line, as in the surviving upper part of the relief, but by an ornamental strip of lotus flowers, leaves and buds among which tadpoles are swimming about. The fragments that have survived from the upper strip show scenes of fishing and dealing with the catch.

33. STATUE OF A MAN

Wood. Height of statue 1.17 m. Sakkara. VIth Dynasty.

A sculpture of similar type to that in Plates 30 and 31. The face is even more stylised perhaps; otherwise in conception and standard of execution the statue is on the same good, average level. Fragments of gesso and paint survive on parts of the body.

34. THE SLAUGHTER OF THE BULL

Detail of a relief on the sarcophagus of Queen Ashayet. Limestone. Height of section 0.56 m. Deir-el-Bahri. XIth Dynasty.

Ashayet was one of the wives of King Mentuhotep I, the founder of the XIth Dynasty. Her sarcophagus was found under the paving stones of Mentuhotep's temple at Deir-el-Bahri. The subject of this intaglio relief was already popular in the Old Kingdom. The drawn outline of the bull is of exceptionally high standard, while the modelling of the bodies of both people and animals, though very fine, is limited to the most important muscles. The change in the canon of proportions is striking. In contrast to the Old Kingdom reliefs, the figures here are taller and slimmer with longer legs and, in proportion to the body, smaller heads. The position of the cow with her sucking calf in the upper strip, which is not divided by any line, creates the impression of a second plane set in perspective, an effect achieved by decreasing the size of this group.

35. THE DWARF SENEB AND HIS FAMILY

Painted limestone. Height 0.33 m. Giza. IVth Dynasty.

This small sculpture is a family portrait of the dwarf, Seneb, who held the post of priest of the funerary cult of Khufu (Cheops) and Djedefre. The sculptor shows all the dwarf's defects—large head, short arms and under-developed legs bearing a thick-set body—with a realism that is almost cruel. The face also, undoubtedly portrays Seneb as he was in life. The modelling of the face and figure of Seneb's wife is more conventional. The relationship between husband and wife is expressed in a manner current in an earlier period. The wife embraces her husband's right shoulder with her right arm, while her left hand rests on his shoulder. (It is interesting that in almost every group of this kind the family relationship is indicated by a gesture on the part of the wife.) The two figures of the children are worth noticing. The little boy and girl are placed at their parents' feet. This is more than a mere aspect of composition. Their posture is conventional, but the realistic vision of the sculptor helped him, perhaps for the first time in the whole of Egyptian sculpture, to model the children in the right proportions, with fat, rounded little bodies. Normally the child in Egyptian art was depicted as a miniature adult.

36. MAN MILKING A COW

Detail of a relief on the sarcophagus of Queen Kawit. Limestone. Height of cow 0.30 m. XIth Dynasty.

This section, adjacent to the scene of the Queen at her toilet in the following reproductions, appears to form part of a sequence of events.

The Queen is drinking from a bowl which the man in this picture has just filled.

The outstanding aspect of this, as of the reliefs on the sarcophagus of Queen Ashayet, is the completely realistic treatment of the outlines of the animals' bodies. The relationship of the human figures to the animals is obviously determined by considerations of composition. Noteworthy is the detail of the hand holding the teat. The calf is tied to the mother's forelegs while she is being milked.

37. QUEEN KAWIT AT HER TOILET

Section of a relief on a limestone sarcophagus. Height of figures 0.35 m. XIth Dynasty.

Queen Kawit, like Ashayet, was a wife of King Mentuhotep I. The reliefs on her sarcophagus are worked in intaglio, in a manner identical to those on Ashayet's sarcophagus. Here, the changes in the canon of proportions of the human figure are even more striking. Note the detail of the hands of the servant-girl adjusting a loose curl in the Queen's wig. Three other curls are held by hair-pins. In view of the precise depiction of movement, reminiscent of the hands of the musicians on a relief in the tomb of Nenkheftikai, the stylised form of the hands here appears almost ornamental. In a similarly stylised manner the Queen is lifting a bowl to her lips with her right hand while with her left she holds a mirror of contemporary design. A servant stands in front of her pouring some liquid into another bowl—probably the milk, as the vessel is identical with the one into which the man in the preceding picture is milking his cow. Behind the servant is a small cupboard with food.

Characteristic of the reliefs on both sarcophagi is the fine summary modelling, the stylisation of details of movement and facial features (the shapes of the eyes are identical with their hieroglyphic symbols), and the new canon of proportions.

38. HEAD OF KING AMENEMHET III

Black basalt. Height 0.35 m. Kom-el-Hisn. XIIth Dynasty.

One of the two well-known portraits of the ruler wearing the White Crown of Upper Egypt (the second, of greenish-black basalt, is in Copenhagen). The two portraits are closely related. They depict the ruler at an early age. The artist of the Cairo portrait modelled the face in a more grandiose manner with smooth surfaces and economical but sure depiction of individual features, while the sculptor of the Copenhagen portrait concentrated on a more precise modelling of detail. The elongated eyes, the broad upper lids and the shape of the mouth, to which a slight upward curve at the corners lends the suggestion of a smile, are common to both portraits.

39. SPHINX OF KING AMENEMHET III

Grey granite. Height 0.63 m. Length 1.24 m. Tanis. XIIth Dynasty.

The royal sphinx with the head framed by a lion's mane instead of the royal wig-cover is a new variation of the official royal portrait during the period of the late XIIth Dynasty. The older type, with the royal ceremonial robes, is first found during the Old Kingdom. The four sphinxes of this type found at Tanis were later 'usurped', that is to say inscribed with the names of later rulers, such as Ramses II, Meneptah and others, and the original inscription removed. The facial features of this sphinx, however, identify it beyond any doubt.

There is a close connexion between this sphinx and the basalt portrait of Amenemhet III in Copenhagen. They are particularly alike in the modelling of the mouth, the nose and the raised cheekbones, as well as in the treatment of the eyebrows and lower lids. The sphinx, although quite small, gives the impression of monumental sculpture.

40. DANCING DWARFS

Ivory. Height of figures 0.07 m. El-Lisht. XIIth Dynasty.

These little figures stand on tiny circular pedestals. As the holes in these pedestals and those in the wood on which the little figures are set correspond, it would seem quite possible that they were toys that could be actuated. The dwarfs would have revolved and pirouetted when the strings that were threaded through the holes were pulled.

The figures are carved with a naturalism similar to that of the family of Seneb. Here, however, it is intensified into caricature, both of form and movement, so much so that it leaves an almost unpleasant impression.

41. THE DAUGHTERS OF DJEHWTYHOTEP

Painted limestone relief. Height 0.81 m. Width 0.75 m. El Bersheh. XIIth Dynasty.

The figures of the two girls, daughters of a high official, Djehwtyhotep, are part of a relief that once adorned the walls of his funerary chapel at El-Bersheh. They are modelled in very low relief. The canon of proportions, the dry graphic handling and the manner of stylisation show a relationship with the reliefs on the sarcophagi of the queens of the XIth Dynasty. The modelling of the body is very summary. From an iconographic point of view the figures do not differ greatly from the female figures on the stelae of the Old Kingdom; even the motif of the lotus flowers which both girls are raising to their noses is the same. The hair-style, with strands twisted at the ends, resembles that of Queen Nefert, the wife of Sesostris II (middle of the XIIth Dynasty). The resemblance is further seen on the jewels worn by the two girls, particularly the pectorals, which enjoyed great popularity during the XIIth Dynasty. They reached their classical form, as shown here, in the middle period. Jewellers probably also fashioned the girls' diadems divided, like their bracelets, into rectangular multi-coloured sections. These are meant to be copies of ribbons, such as those the girls are wearing hanging half-way down their backs, interwoven with rows of lotus flowers and buds.

42. SMALL STATUE OF A HIPPOPOTAMUS

Blue faience. Height 0.10 m. Middle Kingdom.

The blue-green surface of the faience statue is painted with waterflowers and plants. There is even a little bird perched on a papyrus reed. The hippopotamus made frequent appearances in Egyptian art. On reliefs in the tombs of the Old Kingdom we come across scenes representing hippopotamus hunting in the marshy papyrus thickets. These faience figures from the period of the Middle Kingdom may have been successors of these earlier reliefs, although stone carvings of the hippopotamus may be found at a very early period of the Old Kingdom. There are several of these faience statues in museums all over the world. Characteristic of all of them is a humorous regard for the ungainly bulk of this enormous beast.

43—44. AMENEMHET III BEARING OFFERINGS

Upper part of a statue in black granite. Height 1 m. Mit Fares (Faiyum Oasis). XIIth Dynasty.

The period of Amenemhet III saw some novel additions to the accepted types of royal portraiture. One of them is this figure of the king in the guise of a priest presenting offerings, with a heavy wig, a special ceremonial beard, and a leopard skin thrown over his shoulder. On his chest he wears a chain, called a *menat*. The wig is framed by the ends of standards with falcon heads which the king is apparently holding in his hand. The face is similar to that of the sphinx in Plate 39, especially around the mouth. The tightly stretched skin over the cheekbones is strongly marked. The broad stylised line of the eyebrows, lacking in the two preceding portraits, gives the face of this portrait, however, a more severe expression. This type of portrayal, inspired by the ceremonial robes of the cult of the Faiyum priests, shows the Libyan influence, although only in the formal aspects of the work, not in the quality of portrayal.

45. THE QUEEN OF PUNT

Painted limestone relief from the temple of Queen Hatshepsut at Deir-el-Bahri. Size 0.36 m. by 0.82 m. XVIIIth Dynasty.

The relief is part of a vast cycle that adorned the terrace of the queen's temple. Hatshepsut had it carved in celebration of a successful trading expedition to the land of Punt (on the southern shores of the Red Sea). The fragment shows the queen of Punt with a procession of men bearing gifts for the queen of Egypt. Some scholars have suggested that the disfiguring obesity of the queen of Punt was the result of elephantiasis.

46—47. TORSO OF A FEMALE FIGURE

Crystalline limestone. Height 0.84 m. Late XVIIIth Dynasty.

The statue represents the wife of a high official, Khet-min, dressed in rich ceremonial robes of finely pleated, tightly fitting material. She wears a big wig composed of skilfully intertwined strands of hair held by a band of lotus flowers. The hand close to her body grasps a chain *menat*. The face has suffered damage. Details of the almond-shaped eyes with their broad upper lids and elongated outer corners were painted.

48. HEAD OF THE COLOSSAL STATUE OF THUTMOSIS I

Painted sandstone. Height 0.81 m. Karnak. Early XVIIIth Dynasty.

The head is a fragment of a pillar depicting the king as Osiris, the God of the Kingdom of the Dead. This monumental statue dating from the early New Kingdom is completely stylised in form. The broad mouth with its rounded corners, the large eyes, the stylised line of the brows and the summary modelling of the face follow a prescribed pattern with no attempt at delineation of individual features.

49. SPHINX OF QUEEN HATSHEPSUT

Painted limestone. Height 0.62 m. Lentgh 1.08 m. From the queen's temple at Deir-el-Bahri. XVIIIth Dynasty.

This sculpture shows how the artists of the XVIIIth Dynasty copied the sphinx statues typical of the period of Amenemhet III. The queen's delicate face has large, stylised eyes, with the corners and eyebrows elongated by make-up, a pointed chin and a tiny mouth. The same features can be found on the marble statue of the seated queen, now in New York. The surface of the statue still retains fragments of the original polychromy. The lion's body and the pedestal on which it lies are yellow, the man blue, and the pupils of the queen's eyes are red.

The artists of the XVIIIth Dynasty failed, however, to achieve the monumentality of the sphinxes of Amenemhet.

50. STATUE OF AMENHOTEP

Painted limestone. Height 0.73 m. Thebes. XVIIIth Dynasty.

The block statue first appeared at the time of the Middle Kingdom, the subject being a seated male figure with arms crossed over his raised knees, and wrapped in a tightly-fitting cloak. In the course of time the original form became so simplified that the whole body was enclosed in the block, which had rounded edges. The arms were modelled in relief along the top surface, while the body, in a crouching position, was slightly marked out in line along the sides. The smooth sides could thus be engraved with hieroglyphic inscriptions. The five lines of inscription on the statue of Amenhotep are all the more interesting because the name of the dead man was carved on it during the reign of Akhenaton, as the name contains the name of the god, Amon. The face of the statue with its big, clumsy and graphically modelled eyes shows that it was the work of a craftsman of no more than average ability for the period.

51. HEAD OF THE STATUE OF KHET-MIN

Painted crystalline limestone. Late XVIIIth Dynasty.

The head is a fragment of a man's figure on a double statue. The figure of the wife is reproduced in Plates 46 and 47. Although the face has suffered damage, we can see the similarity in style from the overall modelling, the minute details of the wavy strands of the wig and the short fan at the right side of the head.

52. LOWER PART OF THE STATUE OF KING THUTMOSIS III

Dark granite. Height 1.56 m. Karnak. XVIIIth Dynasty.

Statues representing the king bearing offerings are first found during the period of the Middle Kingdom. This fragment is part of a statue similar to the one in Plates 43 and 44. The king, of whose figure only the lower portion has survived, is dressed in pleated ceremonial apron and bears an offering in his outstretched arms. It consists of the fruits of the land of Egypt—ears of corn, lotus flowers, ducks and two quails. The lower part of the statue is carved out of one block, on which the king's legs and the offerings he carries are executed in high relief. The lower part of the block, on the right-hand side, is adorned with ornamentally arranged plants symbolising Lower Egypt and on the other side papyrus clusters, the symbol of the north.

53. HEAD OF QUEEN TIY

Green schist. Height 0.065 m. Found among the ruins of the temple at Serabit el Khadim. XVIIIth Dynasty.

The queen wears a rich wig with tiny locks and a crown bearing the motif of the winged serpent. In the centre between the two uraei on the crown is an oval cartouche with her name. The portrait shows the characteristic features of the queen—the line of the profile with the slightly receding chin, and the small pouting mouth with drooping corners. The same, although rather more sharply outlined, features can be seen in the well-known ebony portrait of the queen in the Berlin Museum. The little Cairo head shows the queen in her youth, almost as a girl, while the ebony head in Berlin is of a mature, even ageing, woman.

54. HEAD OF A COLOSSAL STATUE OF THE GODDESS MUT

Limestone. Height 1.40 m. Late XVIIIth Dynasty.

The goddess's head is covered in a special wig-cover in the form of stylised griffins' wings (the griffin was a bird sacred to the goddess) into which a double crown is set. The modelling of the face resembles that of other statues of gods from the later period of the XVIIIth Dynasty—for instance, the statue of the god Khonsu (Plates 72 and 73) and the head of Amon (Plate 80)—especially in the execution of the eyes. The line of the mouth, with the raised corners suggesting a smile and the striking curve in the centre, is characteristic of some official portraits of Amenhotep III. Egyptian artists returned to those forms after the death of Amenhotep's son, the heretical King Ahkenaton. The statue is sometimes thought to be of Queen Mut Nodjmet, the wife of the last ruler of the XVIIIth Dynasty, King Haremheb.

55. NAOS WITH A STATUETTE OF A WOMAN

Wood. Height 0.61 m. Deir-el-Medina (Thebes). Early XVIIIth Dynasty.

The statuette of a woman in a shrine with a sliding lid is the work of a craftsman of only average skill, but, nevertheless, it gives a good idea of the wooden sculpture of the early XVIIIth Dynasty. A string of blue faience pearls lies over the woman's arm; traces of gesso and pigment remain on parts of the body. This statuette is related to the wooden statue of Rannai in the Pushkin Museum in Moscow, which is dated by its inscription in the period of Thutmosis I. The artistic value of the Moscow statue, however, is incomparably higher.

56—57. HEAD OF A QUEEN

Grey granite. Height 0.50 m. XVIIIth Dynasty.

The queen wears a heavy wig with a diadem in the form of the wings of the sacred griffin, engraved in a stylised version on the surface of the stone. The head of the griffin surmounts the queen's forehead between the two uraei-cobras. The modelling of the face foreshadows the manner of the later Tell-el-Amarna period, particularly in the execution of the eyes. There is the suggestion of a smile about the mouth with its raised corners. In this aspect, the sculpture resembles the official portraits of Amenhotep III. The head has been thought to be of Queen Tiy. However, as it displays none of her facial characteristics, and as the manner of modelling the eyes does not seem possible before the Tell-el-Amarna period, it is perhaps the portrait of a queen from some later period of the XVIIIth Dynasty. The griffins on the crown might justify an identification as Haremheb's wife, Mut Nodjmet.

58. FRAGMENT OF A COLUMN WITH A RELIEF OF KING THUTMOSIS IV

Sandstone. Height 1.51 m. Elephantine. XVIIIth Dynasty.

Three sections have survived from this column on which the king is depicted wearing a blue warrior's crown and holding a bunch of lotus flowers. His head is surmounted by a Horus falcon with outstretched wings. The king's figure is executed in intaglio relief but the conception is idealised. The inscription dates to the period of Ramses II.

59. HEAD OF A WOMAN

Wood covered in gesso and paint. Height 0.30 m. Sakkara. XVIIIth Dynasty.

The head recalls the so-called substitute heads of the Old Kingdom. It is interesting that there is no wig. The skull is slightly elongated at the back. The lower parts of the ear lobes are hidden by big ear-rings painted black. The profile with the long fine aquiline nose is very like the profile of King Thutmosis IV in the previous illustration. The colour of the skin, where the gesso has survived, is pinky-orange. It is not easy to identify this head. The shape of the long neck does not suggest that it was to have been placed on a body made of a different material.

60. WOMAN BEARING OFFERINGS

Fragment of a limestone relief. Size 0.75 m. by 0.36 m. Sakkara. Late XVIIIth Dynasty.

The woman, bearing in her right hand a mat piled high with offerings, is depicted naked, with her body partly covered by her own long hair. The fine modelling of the face and the visible parts of the body, the execution of detail and the fragile beauty of the whole figure recall reliefs from the tomb of Ramose. Like these, it probably originated during the reign of Amenhotep III.

61. HEAD OF A KING

Black granite. Height 0.80 m. Late XVIIIth Dynasty.

Fragment of a statue of a ruler with the head covered in a royal wig-cover (*nemes*), on which the double crown (*pskhent*) has been placed. A ritual beard hides the chin. The face is idealised. From the shape of the eyes, with their thick, almost swollen, upper lids, we might be inclined to place it among the heads of the late XVIIIth dynasty, resembling Tutankhamen. But none of Tutankhamen's features are present, and these, especially around the mouth, are striking. Perhaps it is an ideal portrait of Ay or Haremheb.

62. THE ROYAL SON DRINKING FROM A SACRED COW

Detail of a colossal statue of painted sandstone. Height of cow 2.85 m. Deir-el-Bahri. XVIIIth Dynasty.

This colossal statue once stood in a chapel built by Thutmosis III. The cow is the embodiment of the goddess Hathor, protector of the king. He stands before the cow while his son sucks her milk. Between its horns the animal has a sun disc, the attribute of Hathor, and along the side of the head are papyrus flowers with intertwined stalks. The body is painted a reddy-brown colour with black patches in the shape of clover-leaves. The cartouche on its side is that of Amenhotep II, who in all probability 'usurped' his father's statue.
The statue is carved from one block in an interesting manner that combines free sculpture with high- and bas-relief. A similar method was used for the statue of Thutmosis III presenting offerings (Plate 52).

63. AMENHOTEP, SON OF HAPU

Black granite. Height 1.28 m. Karnak. Late XVIIIth Dynasty.

Amenhotep, son of Hapu, was a famous court official, the architect and vizier of King Amenhotep III. This statue from the temple at Karnak depicts him in the traditional posture of a scribe, sitting cross-legged with a papyrus scroll open on his knees. The right hand is poised, ready to take down dictation; the scribe's tools, including an oblong palette with black and red colours, are flung over his left shoulder. The head is covered in a wig of tiny wavy strands of hair, curled at the ends. The type of wig, the stylised curve of the raised eyebrows, the almond-shaped eyes with elongated outer corners and the beautifully cut mouth are all characteristics of the mannerism of the period of Amenhotep III. The slight inclination of the head gives the face an expression of concentration and thoughtfulness. The fullness of the body is expressed by the folds of skin running symmetrically over the abdomen.

64. AMENHOTEP, SON OF HAPU

Grey granite. Height 1.40 m. Karnak. Late XVIIIth Dynasty.

This is another portrait of King Amenhotep's vizier in old age. Amenhotep is again shown sitting tailor-fashion in the typical posture of a scribe, but here the lower part of his body is covered in a smooth kilt, as worn during the period of the XIIth and early XVIIIth Dynasties. He wears a wig with tiny wavy strands of hair, parted in the middle and brushed back behind the ears. The face bears the marks of old age. The sculptor has concentrated mainly on the mouth and chin, stressing the furrows along the nose and round the corners of the mouth, together with the folds of skin on the face. The mouth itself is finely drawn and defined with a comparatively hard line, as is the modelling of the eyes with the stylised line of the brows.
This portrait of the aging Amenhotep must be one of the most realistic works of art of the late XVIIIth Dynasty prior to the Tell-el-Amarna period. But the means by which this was achieved were somewhat mechanical, and the portrait does not have the depth of some of the portraits of Sesostris III and Amenemhet III.

65. WINGED SPHINX OF KING AMENHOTEP III

Blue faience. Height 0.295 m. Late XVIIIth Dynasty.

A royal sphinx of smaller size with a winged lion's body that departs from the traditional depiction. The king's head is covered with a wig made up of strands of hair marked by strips of white paste. The plaited beard adorning the face is the ceremonial beard of the gods. The

eyes were originally inlaid in a different material. The details were drawn graphically and the deep grooves filled with white paste.
Stylistically, this sphinx is somewhat unusual and would repay closer study. Its small size, the fact that it has wings, a wig instead of a wig-cover, and the beard of the gods suggest that it is not a portrait of a living ruler but a special kind of royal *shabti*.

66. THE KING'S MASTER OF THE STABLES, THAY

Sudanese ebony wood. Height 0.57 m. Sakkara. Late XVIIIth Dynasty.

This small statue was discovered in 1899 wrapped in linen cloth. It was not unwrapped until 1936. It is another typical example of the refined mannerism of the period of Amenhotep III, with is finely worked details of wig and clothing, and the smooth gentle smile of the face. The almond-shaped eyes show a pronounced elongation at the corners. The soft, almost feminine shape of the body can be seen under the tight-fitting garments.
The beautiful, highly groomed male figures from the tomb of Ramose belong to the same group.

67. UNFINISHED HEAD OF QUEEN NEFERTITI

Quartzite. Height 0.33 m. Tell-el-Amarna. XVIIIth Dynasty.

This head, found in one of the houses at Tell-el-Amarna, is a work in the final stages of completion. On the stone, lines have been painted to indicate the shape of the eyes, the curve of the eyebrows and where the head was to have been covered with a wig or crown of different material. The surface of the face is also unfinished here and there. In contrast to the exaggerated manner of the earlier period, the creator of this work has concentrated mainly on the beautiful features of the queen's face. The full mouth with finely modelled lips, the big almond-shaped eyes (here only the edge of the upper lip and the shading of the eyes have been modelled) are the signs of a mature art which had found an assured road to new, spiritually beautiful forms.
(*Note:* The question remains: how was the shading of the eyes to have been completed? This is one of the most remarkable aspects of these unfinished sculptures. A comparison with the beautiful quartz head of a man in the Cairo Museum, which closely resembles the head of Nefertiti in its modelling, suggests that the lines on the unfinished head were meant to indicate an opening to be cut for eyes and eyebrows which would then have been inlaid with different material. If this is so, then, clearly, the dreamy and distinctive expression on the faces of these statues would have been altered completely.)

68. HEAD OF A KING

Obsidian. Height 0.17 m. Karnak. XVIIIth Dynasty.

This head is a fragment from a composite statue made of different materials. The king's face (enlarged in this reproduction) has a smooth surface with barely noticeable transitions. The full mouth with its faintly raised corners and sharply defined lips indicates that the artist was aiming at formal beauty for its own sake rather than at the depiction of individual features. The eyes and eyebrows were inlaid in different material. The head has been identified as that of Thutmosis III, but it is probably of a later period. The modelling of the eyes is closer in style to the time of Amenhotep III. Aldred's assertion that this is a statute of Amenhotep's father, Thutmosis IV, is the most likely.*

* *J. C. Aldred, New Kingdom Art in Egypt, 1951, p. 69*

69. TUTANKHAMEN IN A CHARIOT

Detail of the side of a painted casket from the tomb of Tutankhamen. Height of casket 0.47 m.
Late XVIIIth Dynasty.

The picture was painted on a smooth gesso surface set in an ornamental frame. The scene is of a battle against the Nubians—a battle in which the young ruler could not possibly have taken part. Tutankhamen is wearing a blue warrior's crown and stands in a light, two-wheeled chariot, drawn by two rearing horses. Such a chariot was, in fact, found in his tomb. He is bending a bow at the enemy, and carries on a shoulder strap a big quiver full of arrows which sways against his right hip. Above his head the sun disc is painted with two Uraei bearing the symbol *'nch*, meaning life; at both sides there are griffins of the goddess Nekhbet. Behind the king can be seen a fan carried by Egyptian soldiers. The predominating colours in the picture are warm reds and yellows, with black line drawing.

70. AKHENATON AND HIS FAMILY ENTREATING ATON

Relief in hard limestone. Height 1.05 m. Tell-el-Amarna. XVIIIth Dynasty.

This relief is a fragment from the balustrade of the temple ramp in Akhenaton's one-time capital. It is worked in intaglio in the style characteristic of the early Tell-el-Amarna period. This style, the origin of which was undoubtedly influenced by the king himself, went so far in its striving towards realism that it verged on caricature, stressing and enlarging the negative features of its subjects—as in the case here of Akhenaton himself and the members of his family. On many reliefs and free-standing statues the king is depicted with a long mis-shapen head on a thin neck, full, almost female breasts, a narrow waist, a heavy, flabby abdomen, fat thighs and legs, and weak shins. The figures of the queen and the little princesses show similar signs of deformation, although to a slightly less extent.

The fragment reproduced here shows the king—the founder of the new cult of the god Aton (the sun disc)—worshipping his sun god, which sends out to him and his family rays that terminate in small hands. Two of these are handing to the king and the queen the symbol of life, *'nch*, while they, in their turn, are holding up to the sun sacrificial vessels. The princess holds the symbol *'nch*. On the tables of offerings in front of the king and the queen lie lotus flowers.

71. GOLD MASK OF THE MUMMY OF KING TUTANKHAMEN

Beaten gold, inlaid with coloured glass and semi-precious stones. Valley of the Kings. Late XVIIIth Dynasty.

This mask covered the face of Tutankhamen's mummy, which was protected by three coffins, one inside the other. The mask is made of beaten gold, highly polished, the detail being picked out with inlays of glass and semi-precious stones. The king's wig-cover is inlaid with glass, the colour of lapis lazuli. His necklace is composed alternately of cornelians, lapis lazuli and green feldspar; the whites of his eyes are in limestone and the iris in obsidian.

The young king wears a long plaited beard, symbol of Osiris, with its end curled up. This, also, is inlaid with glass the colour of lapis lazuli. The heads of the sacred griffin and cobra (Uraeus) tower above his forehead.

The mask is both a specimen of the exquisite craftsmanship of the Egyptian jewellers and an outstanding work of sculpture. The rich materials do not in the least distract attention from its persuasive qualities as portraiture.

72—73. STATUE OF THE GOD KHONSU

Grey granite. Height 2.52 m. Late XVIIIth Dynasty.

Khonsu was a member of the Thebes Triad, son of Amon-Re and his goddess-wife, Mut. He is depicted as a youth, his immaturity being shown by the side-lock of childhood, a thick plait worn on the right side of the head. In his right hand he is holding the flail and systrum, in his left a sceptre. In spite of his youth, he wears the beard of the gods. The workmanship dates the statue to the very end of the XVIIIth Dynasty. The shape of the mouth recalls the portrait of Tutankhamen.

74. MARCHING SOLDIERS

Painted limestone relief. Height 0.63 m. Width 1.43 m. XVIIIth Dynasty.

At the head of the battalion march men bearing standards and fans, followed by soldiers armed with shields, lances and short, sickle-shaped knives. The relief is a fragment of a larger strip. Of the upper section above the inscription only part of the surface of the water has survived; the lower strip shows boats and figures of boatmen.

75. PTAH-MAY AND HIS WIFE TIY

Relief on a limestone block. Size 0.60 m. by 0.90 m. Sakkara. Late XVIIIth Dynasty.

Ptah-May was the chief jeweller and weaver at Aton's temple in Memphis during the first years of Akhenaton's reign. The relief depicts the deceased and his wife in a traditional manner seated in front of a table with offerings. In style, the relief is a mixture of features from the Tell-el-Amarna period (the silhouette of the figure) and the mannerism of the preceding one (the modelling of the face).

76. BUST OF A QUEEN

Wood covered with gesso and paint. Height 0.77 m. Late XVIIIth Dynasty.

The face of this girl, full of charm, clearly indicates that she is a member of the family of Akhenaton. The full, beautifully cut lips and the round, slightly projecting little chin remind one of Queen Nefertiti and of the well-known heads of the princesses. The crown with the Uraeus resembles that of Nefertiti, known from the relief and bust in the Berlin Museum. The bust is also related to the little statues of Tutankhamen—the drawing of the eyes is identical with the heads on the lids of his funerary vessels. This is probably a portrait of one of Akhenaton's daughters, perhaps Princess Ankhes-en-amon, the wife of Tutankhamen.

77. HEAD OF A COLOSSAL STATUE OF A KING

Painted quartzite. Height of statue 3.00 m. Medinet Habu. Late XVIIIth Dynasty.

The face of this young ruler (considerably damaged in the upper section) again recalls the face of Tutankhamen, especially in the part around the mouth. It undoubtedly represents either him or his elder brother, Smenkh-ka-ra. After the death of Tutankhamen it was usurped by Ay, and then by Haremheb.

78. SEATED SCRIBE

Detail of a limestone relief. Height 0.65 m. Sakkara. Late XVIIIth or early XIXth Dynasty.

This is a detail from a relief decorating the tomb of Yenuia. The scribe, squatting on his right heel, is raising a scroll in a somewhat artificial manner and turning his head towards the person who is dictating to him. The outline of the figures shows the influence of the Tell-el-Amarna style, although the execution is very inept. This is particularly apparent on the column of hieroglyphics.

79. WOMAN WORSHIPPING THE GODDESS HATHOR

Painted limestone relief. Size 0.78 m. by 0.69 m. New Kingdom.

This section of the relief depicts Sat, the deceased, standing with raised arms in front of a table of offerings. These offerings and the gesture of worship are intended for the goddess Hathor, who is not shown in this section. The summary and superficial execution is plain in the hand of the deceased, where the fingers are not marked at all, and in the column of hieroglyphics, which are literally scratched on the surface.

80. HEAD OF A STATUE OF AMON

Quartzite. Height 0.18 m. Karnak. Late XVIIIth Dynasty.

In type and treatment this head is related to the statue of Khonsu (Plates 72 and 73). It was probably executed during Tutankhamen's reign, and, like the statue of Khonsu, reproduces some of the features of the young ruler.

81. STATUETTE OF A WOMAN

Wood. Height 0.43 m. XIXth Dynasty.

The statuette shows an unknown woman in a long, tight-fitting garment, with a long wig. The small heart-shaped face with its enormous stylised eyes and tiny mouth with deepened corners has something of the sweetness of expression found in some of the statues of the reign of Ramses II.

82. STATUETTE OF THE LADY HENOUTOU

Wood. Height 0.22 m. Sakkara. XIXth Dynasty.

The Lady Henoutou wears a big wig surmounted by a crown with uraei-serpents. She is dressed in a softly flowing, pleated garment. Her hand, held against her breast, is grasping a bunch of flowers. The change in the canon of proportions is interesting: note the big head, enlarged even further by the wig, the long body and little short legs. The statuette is an example of a very high level of craftsmanship.

83. DETAIL OF THE RELIEF DECORATING THE SECOND COFFIN OF TUTANKHAMEN.

Relief incised into gold foil on a thin layer of gesso. Average height of figures 0.69 m. Late XVIIIth Dynasty.

The relief formed part of the decorations of the back panel of Tutankhamen's second coffin. It serves as an illustration to the inscription containing the words the deceased was to address to the guardians of the Third Gate of the Underworld (Chapter 147 of the Book of the Dead). These guardians are depicted by the artist as zoomorphic gods, the first with a bull's head, the second with that of a ram.

84. MOURNING WOMEN

Fragment of a relief on the tomb of Kyiry. Limestone. Size 0.95 m. by 0.55 m. Sakkara.

Late XVIIIth or early XIXth Dynasty.

A group of mourning women, part of a funeral cortège, is shown. The mourning is expressed by the gestures of the hands, some raised above the head, others held to the face. Expressions of grief may be seen on some of the faces. The heads of the oxen on the left belong, perhaps, to the team drawing the hearse.

85—86. RAMSES II QUELLING AN UPRISING

Painted relief on a limestone block. Size of block 1.00 m. by 0.50 m. by 0.88 m. Temple of Ptah at Memphis.

XIXth Dynasty.

This scene, in intaglio relief, is much the same as that in Narmer's palette at the very beginning of Egyptian history. The king, with a blue warrior's crown on his head and an axe in his left hand, holds three conquered enemies by the hair. Their physiognomy and colour (red, yellow and black) reveal their race. The superiority of the king is emphasised, as in the earlier periods, by his larger size.

87. MAN POURING LIQUID INTO A JUG

Limestone. Height of relief 0.65 m. Sakkara. Late XVIIIth or early XIXth Dynasty.

Another section of the relief decorating the tomb of Yenuia, Sakkara. The man's movements, as he carefully pours a liquid from one big jug into another, are interesting. In execution, the detail resembles that of the figure of the seated scribe in Plate 78, and is an example of the kind of craftsmanship produced by the Memphis school at the end of the XVIIIth or the beginning of the XIXth Dynasty.

88—90. COLOSSAL STATUE OF SETI I

Alabaster. Height 2.38 m. Karnak. XIXth Dynasty.

This statue, carved from a material rarely used by the Egyptian sculptors, is made up of several independently worked parts. (A join may be seen at the wrists.) In the modelling of the face the sculptor followed the tradition of the 'beautiful' heads of the late Tell-el-Amarna period, but the transitions are smoother and the individual features not so expressive. The stylised eyes were inlaid with different material. The grooves at the corners of the mouth must have been deepened with a drill. The statue was damaged in its lower parts and restored with an unsuitable shape of ceremonial apron.

91. BUST OF KING RAMSES II

Grey granite. Height of fragment 0.77 m. Tanis. XIXth Dynasty.

The upper part of a statue of the king in ceremonial court costume. The smooth undergarment is pleated along the edges of the sleeves and partly hidden under the pleated drapery laced up over the right arm. The king wears a wig of tiny curls held by a diadem similar to that found in the tomb of Tutankhamen. Among Tutankhamen's jewels was also a bracelet with the sacred falcon, Horus, such as the king wears here on his wrist. Ramses' face has a youthful look; it is softly modelled and the eyes are artificially prolonged at the outer corners with the line of the brows stylised. The small mouth with the deep expressive grooves at the corners gives the face a gracious, smiling expression.

92. STATUETTE OF THE LADY RES

Wood with gesso and paint. Height 0.32 m. XVIIIth Dynasty.

The Lady Res, like the Lady Henoutou, is depicted wearing a heavy wig and dressed in pleated, softly flowing robes. She holds a lotus flower in her left hand. The catalogue of the Cairo Museum reveals that the statuette was found at Tell-el-Amarna. The execution is summary; nevertheless, the shape of the eyes and the small, pouting mouth vaguely recall the portrait of Queen Tiy.

93. RELIGIOUS DANCE AT A FUNERAL

Limestone relief. Height 0.40 m. Sakkara. XIXth Dynasty.

The scene depicts a religious dance during a funeral. The men form an independent group in the right half of the picture. They are walking in rows of three behind the two leaders, one of whom holds a sceptre. Their hands are raised in a gesture of adulation. The left half of the relief is taken up by a group of dancing women dressed in long transparent robes and beating small drums. Two girls are dancing with castanets. The sculptor has shown only the upper part of the figures in the second plane. The emotions expresssed by the agitated gestures are undoubtedly an inheritance from the Tell-el-Amarna period.

94. PRISONERS

Painted limestone relief. Height 0.70 m. Width 0.75 m. XIXth Dynasty.

This fragment depicts a group of foreign prisoners tied together by the hair. The group is interesting by reason of its ornamental composition constructed symmetrically along a central axis. The figures along this axis are shown *en face*, the others, to the right and the left, in profile, with partially overlapping contours. The frame is formed by the raised hands of the prisoners.

95. GROUP OF MEN IN A FUNERAL PROCESSION

Section of a painted limestone relief. Height 0.75 m. Thebes. XIXth Dynasty.

A group of men accompanying a hearse is shown. The first in the row is a shaven priest holding a short fan; in the second row is a scribe with a scroll of papyrus. The first two figures are dressed in shirt-like garments with shoulder straps; the others are wrapped in full cloaks. The sculptor has succeeded in creating an effect of deep perspective in the figures in the front row (and in others not included in this representation) by a gradual decrease in the size of their heads. The large patches and clear-cut lines make this relief unusually effective.

96. BUST OF A PRINCESS

Limestone. Height 0.73 m. Gurnah. IXth Dynasty.

This partly preserved statue, found in the ruins of the Ramesseum at Gurnah, is undoubtedly a portrait of one of the princesses at the court of Ramses II. The young woman wears a heavy, intricately plaited wig held by a diadem with two uraei. The wig is surmounted by a tall crown made up of the bodies of sacred cobras. A broad chain, made up of hieroglyphic symbols for the word *Nfr* (Nefer), adorns her chest and shoulders. The smooth dress, fitting tightly over the left breast, is marked with an engraved rosette. The hand lying against the breast is holding a *menat* chain, with a pendant in the shape of a female figure. The heart-shaped face resembles those of the granite statues of Ramses II, especially in the modelling of the tiny mouth with its deeply grooved corners. The almond-shaped eyes are strikingly extended at the outer corners.

97. THE SCRIBE HAPI

Red sandstone. Height 0.70 m. Early XIXth Dynasty.

The scribe is seated on a circular cushion in a somewhat unusual posture, with his hand holding a scroll of papyrus supported on the raised left leg. He is dressed in a long garment with a pleated kilt, and wears a wig fashionable at the time of Amenhotep III.

The mannerism of the Amenhotep period may be seen in the modelling of the face. The statue dates from the very late XVIIIth or early XIXth Dynasty.

98—99. THAY AND HIS SISTER NAIA

Limestone. Height 0.90 m. Late XVIIIth or early XIXth Dynasty.

This group depicts, in traditional manner, Thay and his sister-wife, Naia. They are sitting in a relaxed pose side by side on a seat with a tall back-rest, reminiscent of those found in the sculptures of the Old Kingdom. The wigs and the modelling of the faces recall the mannerism of the period of Amenhotep III, as does the soft fullness of Thay's figure with its emphasis on the folds of skin across his abdomen. The group may have originated in the late XVIIIth or the very beginning of the XIXth Dynasty.

100. TORSO OF A STATUE OF AN UNKNOWN KING

Fine hard limestone. Height 0.70 m. Karnak. XIXth Dynasty.

The king is dressed in a tight tunic, its surface decorated with thick, scale-like feathers. The finely pleated kilt is held by a decorative belt. The torso, representing an ideal type of male figure of the late XVIIIth or early XIXth Dynasty, is a highly accomplished masterpiece.

101—102. SECTION OF THE RELIEF FROM THE TOMB OF MAY

Limestone. Height 1.85 m. Sakkara. XIXth Dynasty.

The section shows two scenes one above the other. In the upper strip the seated scribe is checking a list of prisoners. In the lower one another scribe is standing and recording herds of cattle. Dominating all is the large figure of the deceased watching the scene. (The reproduction here includes only his hand, which holds a tall staff.)

Plate 102 shows a detail of the upper strip of the relief—the figure of the seated scribe.

103. SACRIFICE BEARERS

Section of a relief. Painted limestone. Size 0.65 m. by 1.33 m. XXth Dynasty.

The section shows one of a row of shaven-headed men in long kilts which recall those of the Old Kingdom. In his left hand the man holds bunches of lotus blossoms, in the right a young crane. The graphic and dry modelling is typical of the later period of the New Kingdom.

104. HARMAKHIS, SON OF KING SHABAKA

Quartzite. Height 0.66 m. Karnak. XXVth Dynasty.

Shabaka, the son of a king of Nubian origin, was the first prophet of Amon.

In the late period the artists deliberately returned to the style of the Old Kingdom, copying not only the posture and dress but also the canon of proportions of the human figure.

105. WORSHIPPING THE GODDESS SAKHMET

Painted limestone relief. Size 0.90 m. by 1.17 m. XIXth Dynasty.

This fragment of a relief depicts the deceased, Amenemint, and his family, worshipping the Egyptian goddess of war, Sakhmet. Amenemint is holding a lotus flower in his left hand and a papyrus stalk in his right. Behind him stands his wife with her hands raised in a gesture of adoration. On top of her head is a cone of fragrant unguent.

The third figure, a child, also holds a papyrus plant. The goddess of war is depicted, in traditional manner, as a woman with a lion's head. From the fine modelling of detail and the style of the garments we may place the relief in the period of the late XVIIIth or early XIXth Dynasty

106. SCENE FROM THE BOOK OF THE DEAD

Painting on papyrus. XXIst Dynasty.

A copy of a book made for Ta-nefer, the third prophet of Amon. The deceased kneels in an attitude of worship before the god, who has the shape of a ram with a treble crown on his head. Above him rises a winged uraeus, the goddess Wadjyt. In front sits a small figure, the goddess of truth (Maat), depicted in the hieroglyphic abbreviation current at the time, with an ostrich feather on her head. The deceased, too, wears a crown of ostrich feathers. In front of him on the ground stand four vessels, each containing a plume of four ostrich feathers, the symbol of the goddess of Truth.

107. DETAIL FROM THE RELIEF ON THE STELE OF AMENEMINT

Limestone. Sakkara. XIXth Dynasty.

This shows a procession of men and women carrying offerings and gifts. It forms the lower strip of the stele of Amenemint (Plate 109).

108. KING OSORKON LAUNCHING A SACRED BARGE

Limestone. Height 0.18 m. XXIIIrd Dynasty.

Osorkon III, a ruler of the XXIIIrd, the Libyan, Dynasty, is depicted during the solemn rite of the launching of a barge dedicated to Amon. Of this tiny statuette only the figure of the king has survived. He kneels on his left knee in profound adoration; he is dressed in a kilt and ceremonial apron of the old-fashioned type in use in the later period of the XVIIIth Dynasty. Only a fragment of the barge has survived. The statuette was probably a votive offering to the temple on the occasion of the consecration of the new barge. The king's kilt and wig-cover still show the remnants of the red used as a foundation for gilding.

109. STELE OF AMENEMINT

Limestone. Height 1.47 m. Width 1.05 m. Sakkara. Probably XIXth Dynasty.

An edge projecting at right-angles forms a frame to this stele. On the vertical parts a hieroglyphic text is inscribed, which, in this case, also serves an ornamental purpose. The upper, horizontal, part is decorated with symmetrically composed scenes of worship of the god Anubis and the goddess Hathor. The actual surface of the stele is horizontally divided into two strips. The upper one is composed symmetrically along the axis and depicts the deceased and his wife worshipping the god Osiris (left) and the god Horus (right). The lower strip shows a traditional scene with a procession of men and women presenting offerings. The seated pair, the details of the garments and the execution point to the late XVIIIth or early XIXth Dynasty.

110. MOURNING WOMAN

Detail of a limestone relief. XXth Dynasty.

Figure of a woman with her hands raised to her head. The intaglio relief is carved in a cursory manner.

111, 113. STATUE OF ROMA ROY

Limestone. Height 1.05 m. XXIst Dynasty.

A block statue depicting a seated man with hands crossed on raised knees and wrapped tightly in a cloak. The type of block statue seen here became established in the early XVIIIth Dynasty. The seated figure is modelled only roughly by picking out the curved parts of the block, to which inscriptions were affixed.

112. STATUE OF ROMA ROY

Grey granite. Height 1.05 m. XXIst Dynasty.

The statue is executed in the way described above, but in a different material. The details of the face, especially the summary modelling of the eyes, suggest that both statues were the work of one artist.

114. SCENE OF SACRIFICE FROM THE BOOK OF THE DEAD

Painting on papyrus. Height of figure 0.195 m. XXIst Dynasty.

The scene is taken from Ta-Nefer's Book of the Dead. The deceased, wrapped in a loose cloak, stands in front of a table with offerings. In his left hand he holds a censer, in his right a small ewer from which he is pouring a libation. The theme of libation is a conventional one and is repeated in all the Books of the Dead without variation.

115. KNEELING MAN AND WIFE

Detail of a painted limestone relief. Height 0.23 m. Width 0.20 m. Deir-el-Medina. XXth Dynasty.

This fragment probably formed part of the upper edge of a stele. The figures are depicted in an attitude of worship, with outstretched arms. The man kneels on his right knee with his left leg stretched out behind. His wife, Taweret, is kneeling behind him. A similar scene of worship forms part of the upper portion of the stele of Amenemint (Plate 109).

116. HERUBEN DRINKING FROM THE SOURCE OF LIVING WATER

Painting on papyrus. Height 0.235 m. XXIst Dynasty.

Scene from the Book of the Dead of the Lady Heruben. The deceased kneels on the bank of the river and, leaning on her arm, bends her head down to the edge of the water. She is dressed in a white garment with a belt; strands of hair fall over her forehead and back and cover the nape of her neck. The drawing is executed with clean and vivid draughtsmanship. The reproduction here shows only the right-hand half of the scene. On the left, on the other side of the stream, is a crocodile drawn with equal liveliness.

117. HEAD OF MENTUEMHET

Black granite. Height 0.50 m. Karnak. XXVth Dynasty.

Mentuemhet was a well-known official in Thebes during the reign of King Taharka. He came from a noble family and held the office of fourth prophet of Amon. He was instrumental in the rebuilding of Thebes after the devastation caused by the invasion of Assurbanipal. His virtues are recorded for all time on the relief in the temple at Karnak.

The bust is a fragment of one of his statues, and is an undoubted masterpiece. The face is unmistakably a portrait. The ageing man with his coarse features and little eyes set in his puffed-up face is a work of the most convincing realism and compositional skill.

EARLY PERIOD:

Ist and IInd Dynasty . . . . 3197—2779 B. C.
Kings: Ist Dynasty: *Menes* (*Narmer*)
IInd Dynasty: *Khasekhem*

OLD KINGDOM:

IIIrd Dynasty . . . . 2778—2723
Kings: *Zoser*
IVth Dynasty . . . . 2723—2563
Kings: *Snefru*, *Khufu*, *Khafre*, *Menkawre*
Vth Dynasty . . . . 2563—2424
Kings: *Veserkaf*, *Sahure*, *Neferkare*, *Niuserre*, *Asosi*, *Venis*
VIth Dynasty . . . . 2423—?
Kings: *Teti*, *Veserkare*, *Pepy I*, *Menenre*, *Pepy II*

FIRST PERIOD OF DECLINE:

VIIth—Xth Dynasties . . . . ?—2134

MIDDLE KINGDOM

XIth Dynasty . . . . 2134—2000
Kings: *Enyotef*, *Mentuhotep I—V*
XIIth Dynasty . . . . 2000—1785
Kings: *Amenemhet I* (2000—1970), *Senusret I* (*Sesostris I*) (1980—1935), *Amenemhet II* (1938—1903), *Senusret II* (*Sesostris II*) (1906—1887), *Senusret III* (*Sesostris III*) (1887—1849), *Amenemhet III* (1849—1801), *Amenemhet IV* (1801—1792), *Sebeknefrure* (1792—1785).

SECOND PERIOD OF DECLINE

XIIIth—XVIth Dynasties . . . . 1785—1590

NEW KINGDOM:

XVIIth Dynasty . . . . 1680?—1580

XVIIIth Dynasty . . . . 1576—1347

Kings: *Ahmose I* (1576—1554) *Amenhotep I* (1553—1526), *Thutmosis I* (1526—1511), *Thutmosis II* (1511—1501), *Hatshepsut* (1511—1480), *Thutmosis III* (1501—1447), *Amenhotep II* (1448—1412), *Thutmosis IV* (1412—1402), *Amenhotep III* (1402—1365), *Amenhotep IV* (*Akhenaton*) (1373—1357), *Smenkh-ka-ra* (before 1357), *Tutankhamen* (*Tutankhaton*) (1357—1349), *Ay* (1349—1347).

XIXth Dynasty . . . . 1347—1205

Kings: *Haremheb* (1347—1319), *Ramses I* (1319—1318), *Seti I* (1318—1298), *Ramses II* (1298—1232), *Mernaptah*, *Amenmesse*, *Siptah*, *Seti II* (1232—1205)

XXth Dynasty . . . . 1200—1090

Kings: *Setkhnakhte* (1200—1198), *Ramses III* (1198—1166), *Ramses IV—XI* (1166—1085).

LATE PERIOD:

XXIst Dynasty . . . . 1085—950

Kings: *The Theban High Priests of Amon*

XXIInd Dynasty . . . . 950—730

Kings of Libyan Origin: *Sheshonk I—V*, *Osorkon I—IV*, *Takelot I—II*

XXIIIrd Dynasty . . . . .817?—730

XXIVth Dynasty . . . . 730—715

XXVth Dynasty . . . . 715—656

Kings of Nubian Origin: *Piankhi*, *Shabaka*, *Shabataka*, *Takarka*, *Tanutamon*

XXVIth Dynasty . . . . 663—525

Saite Dynasty. Kings: *Psammetek I* (663—609), *Nekav* (609—594), *Psammetek II* (594—588), *Vahibre* (588—568), *Ahmose* (568—525), *Psammetek III* (*525*)

XXVIIth Dynasty . . . . 525—404

First period of Persian Rule

XXVIIIth Dynasty . . . . 404—398

XXIXth Dynasty . . . . 398—378

XXXth Dynasty . . . . 378—341

Second Persian occupation of Egypt

Alexander the Great of Macedonia invaded Egypt in the year 332 B. C.

PLATES

1

2

3

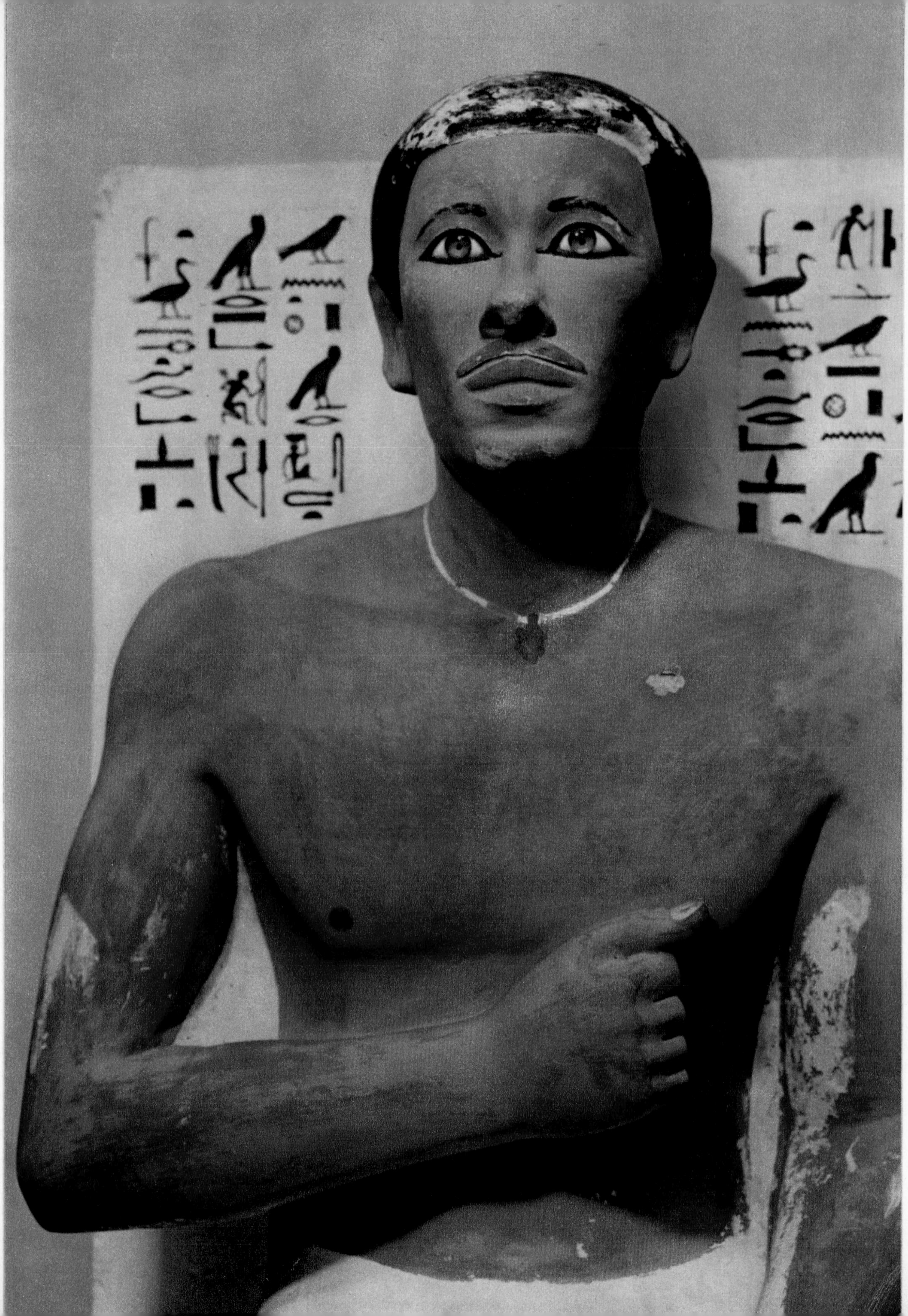

4

5

6 7

8

9

10

12

13

14

15

16 17

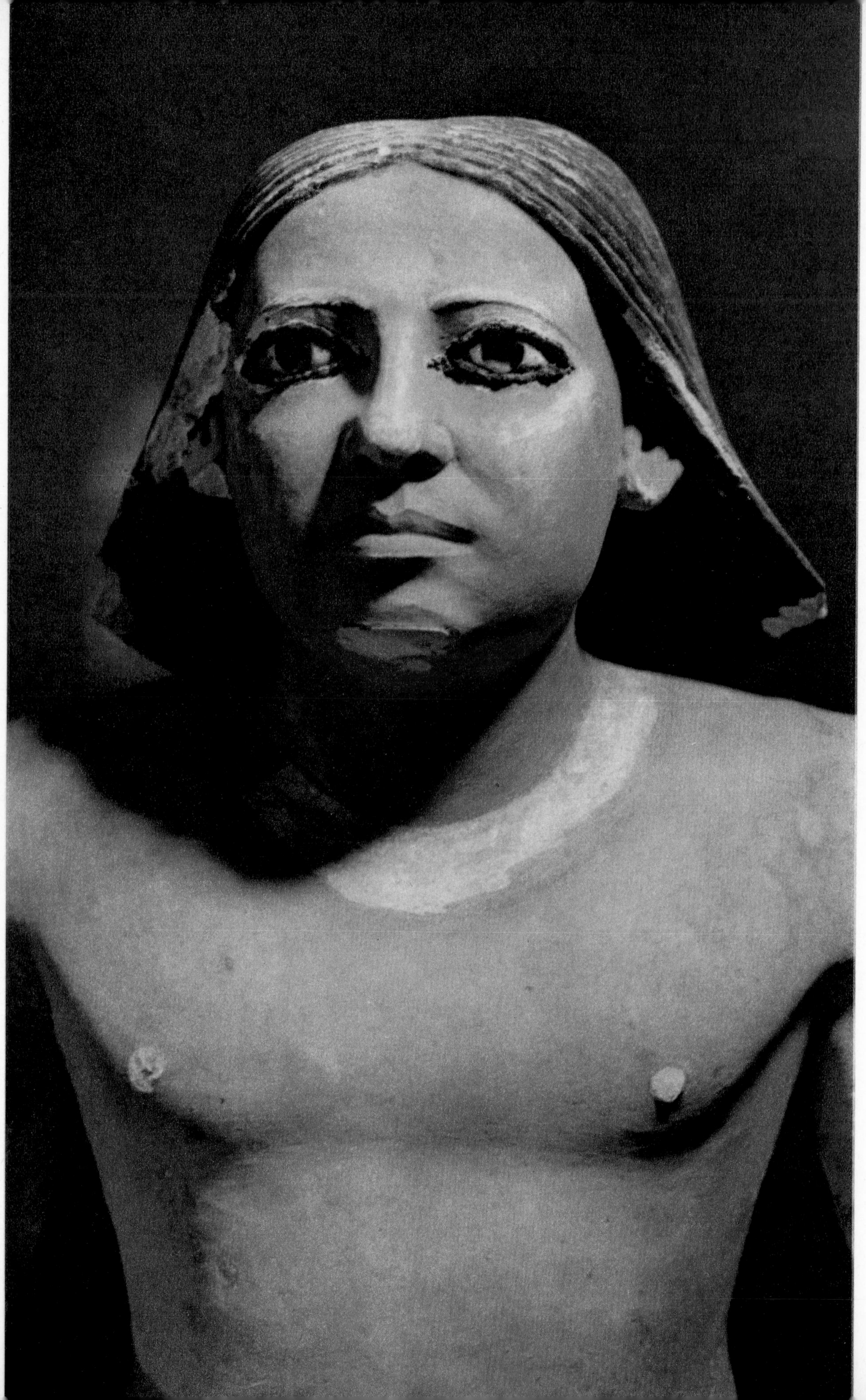

22

23

24

1533

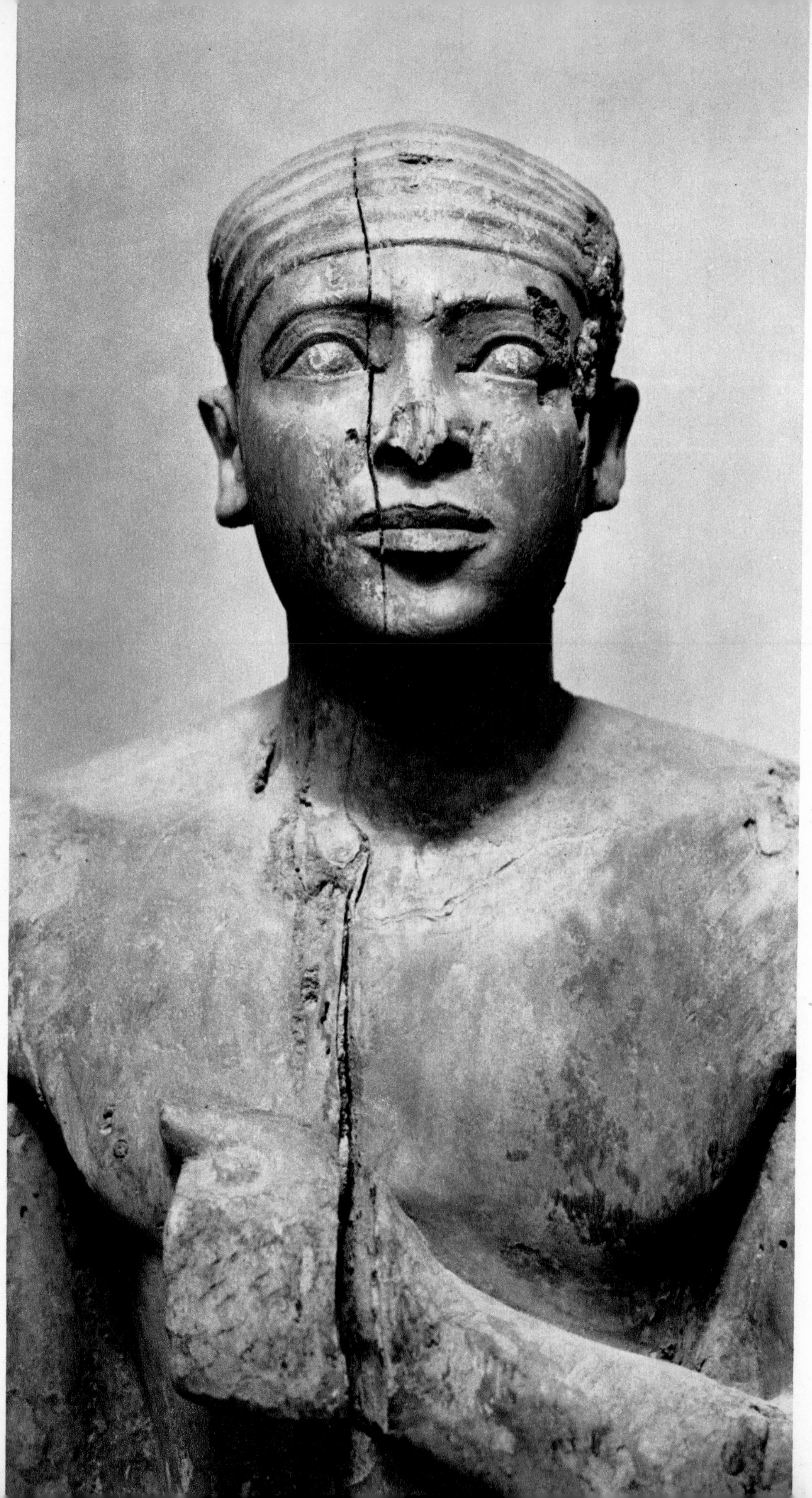

30

31

36

41

47

52

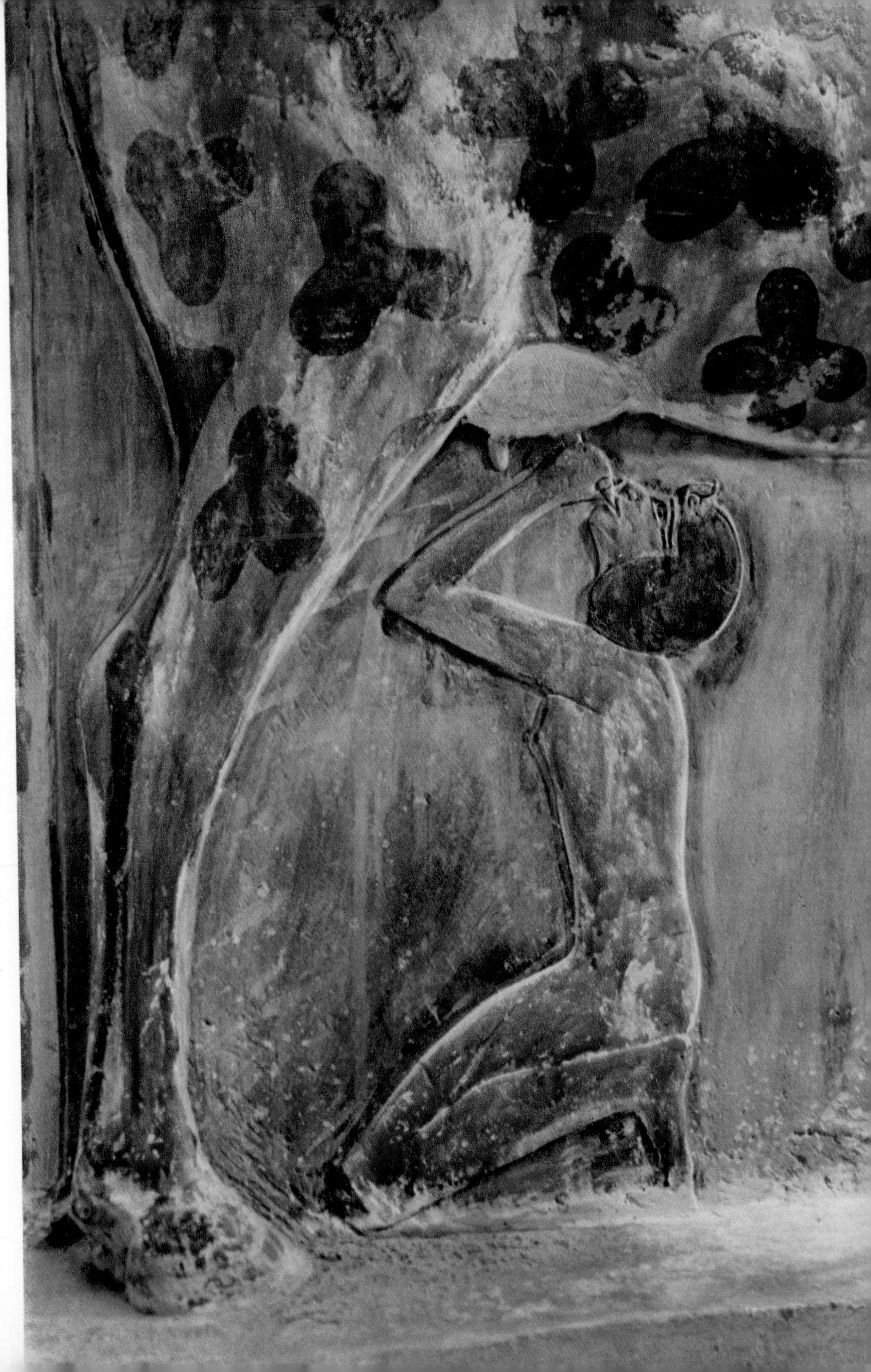

65

66

68

72

82

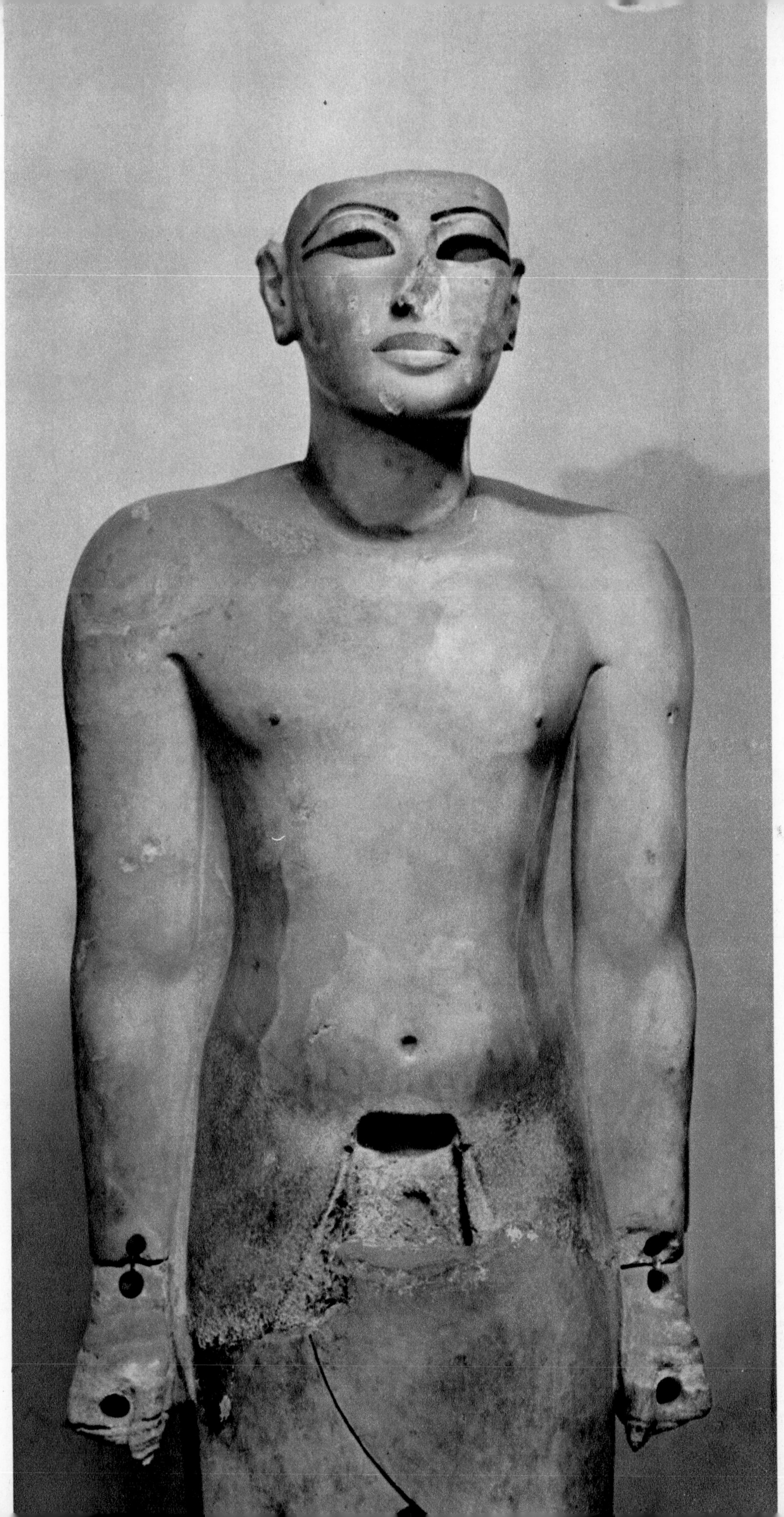

88

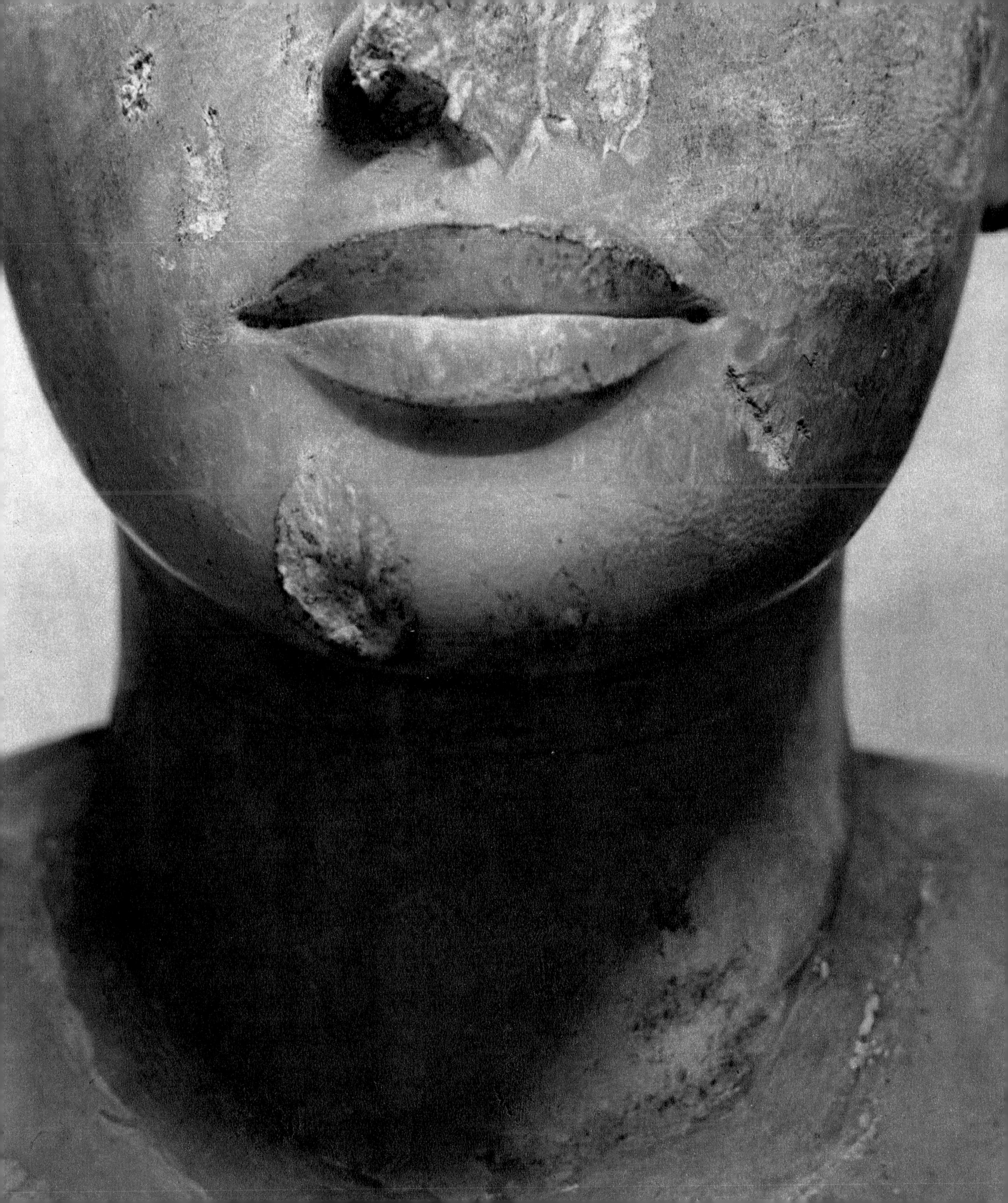

93

97

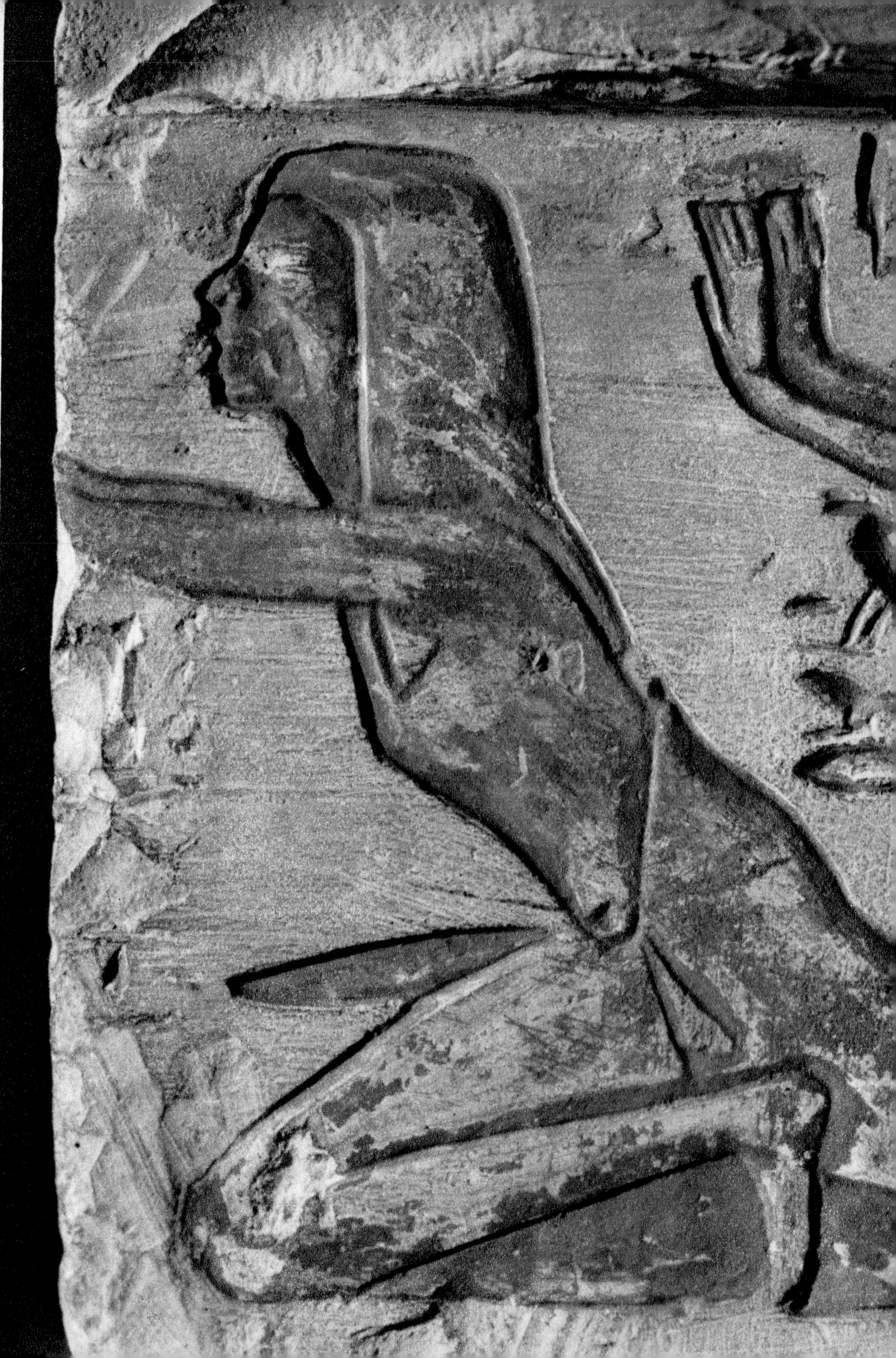